I AM GRATEFUL TO GOD, OUR FATHER FOR
EVERYTHING. I BELIEVE THAT THE MEANING OF LIFE
IS TO GIVE MEANING TO OTHER LIVES LIKE YOURS.
YOU ARE AND MAKE SENSE OF MINE.

LOV U

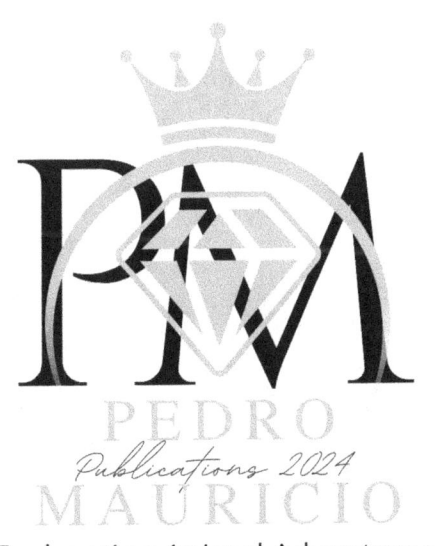

PEDRO
Publications 2024
MAURICIO

Enchanting Animal Adventures:
A Whimsical Coloring Journey

This book belongs to :

_____

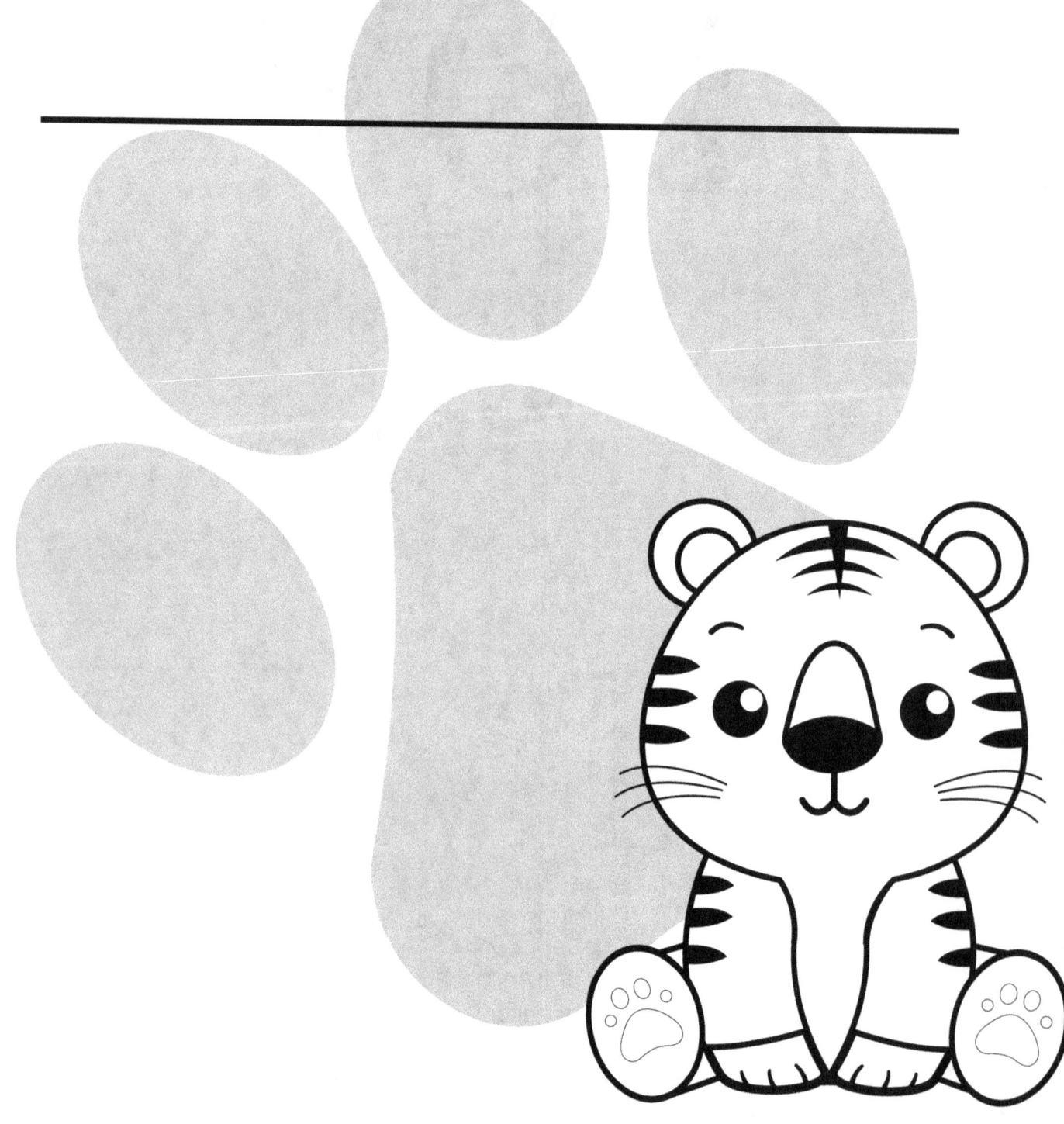

TEST COLORS

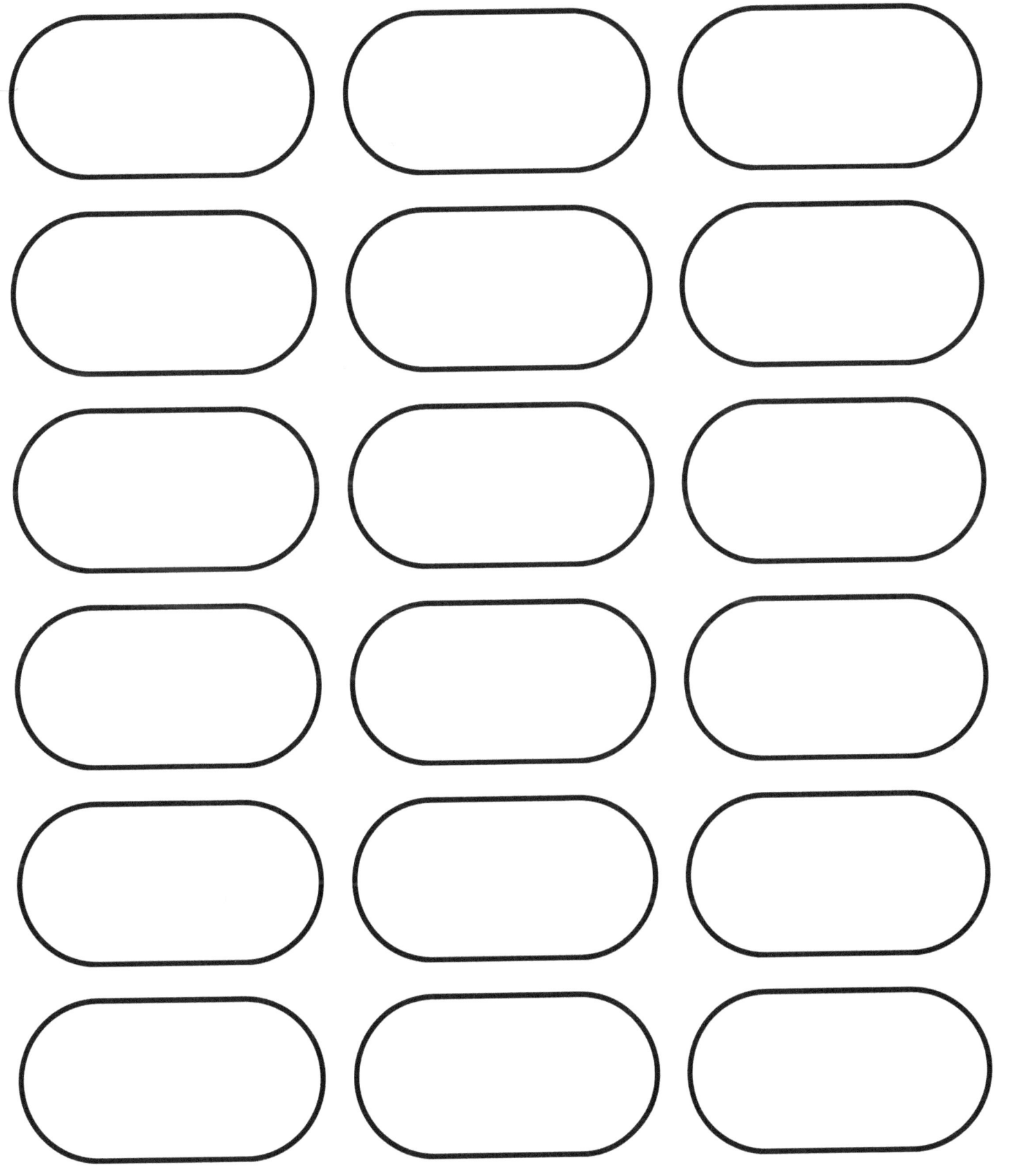

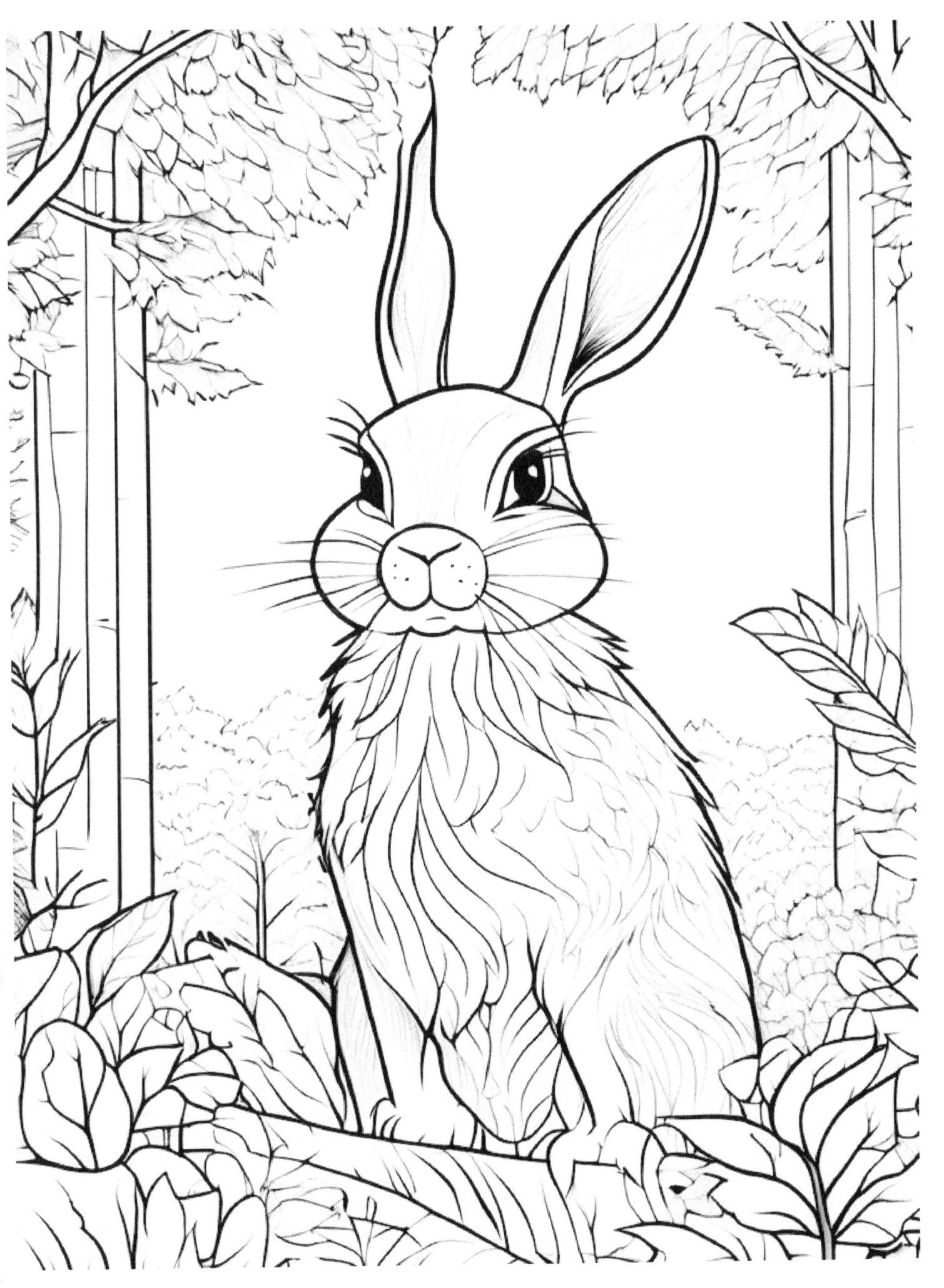

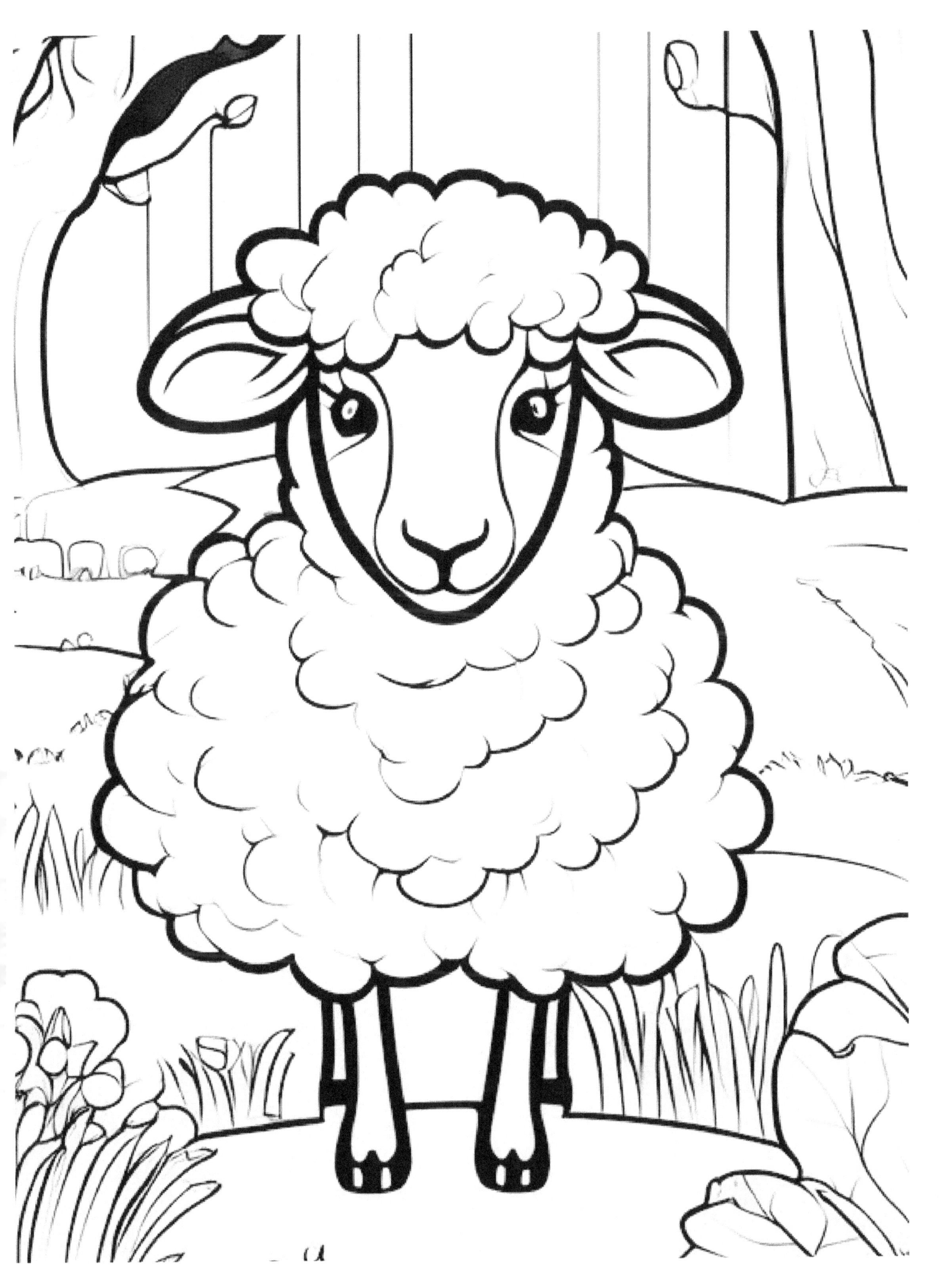

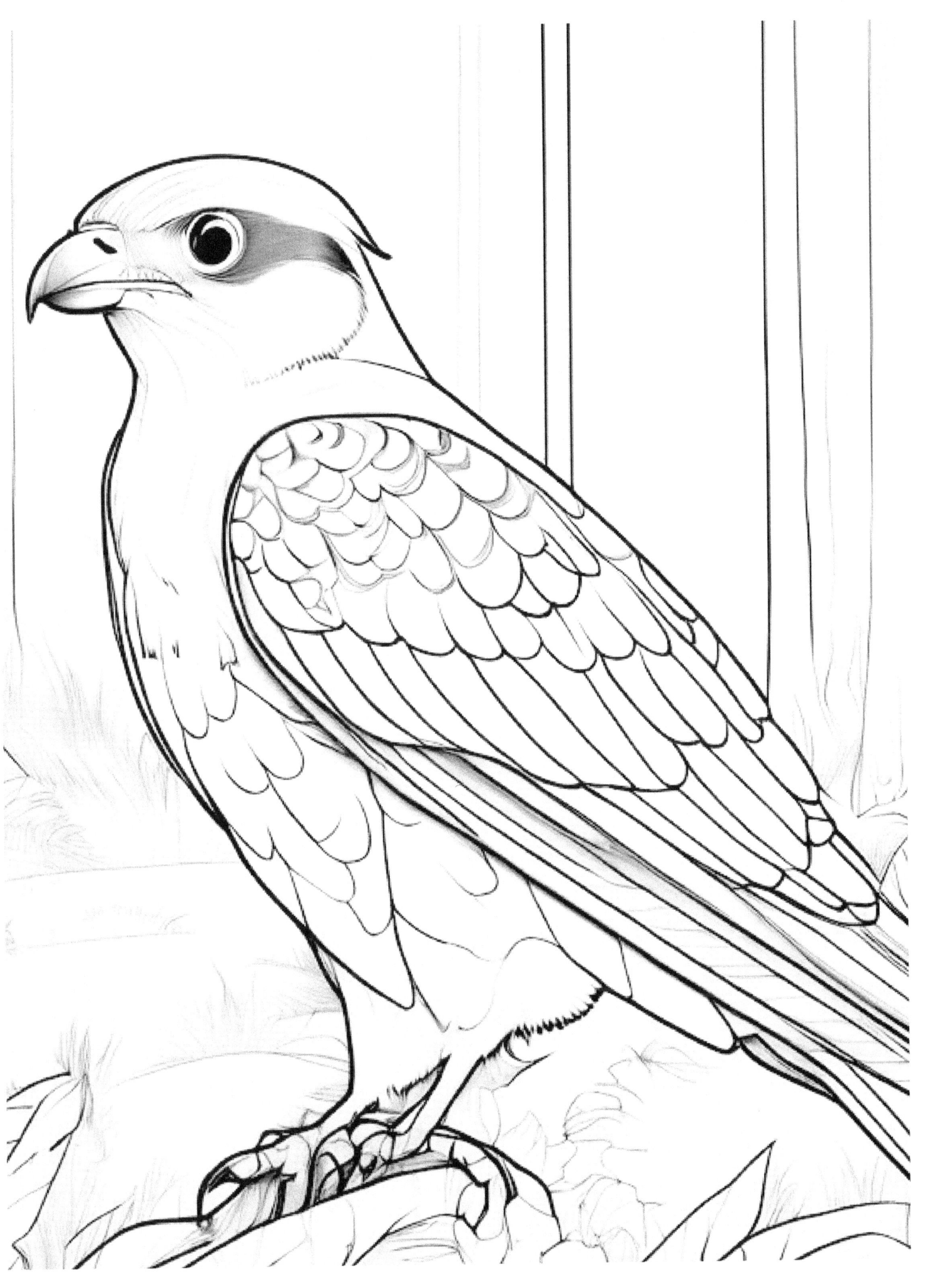

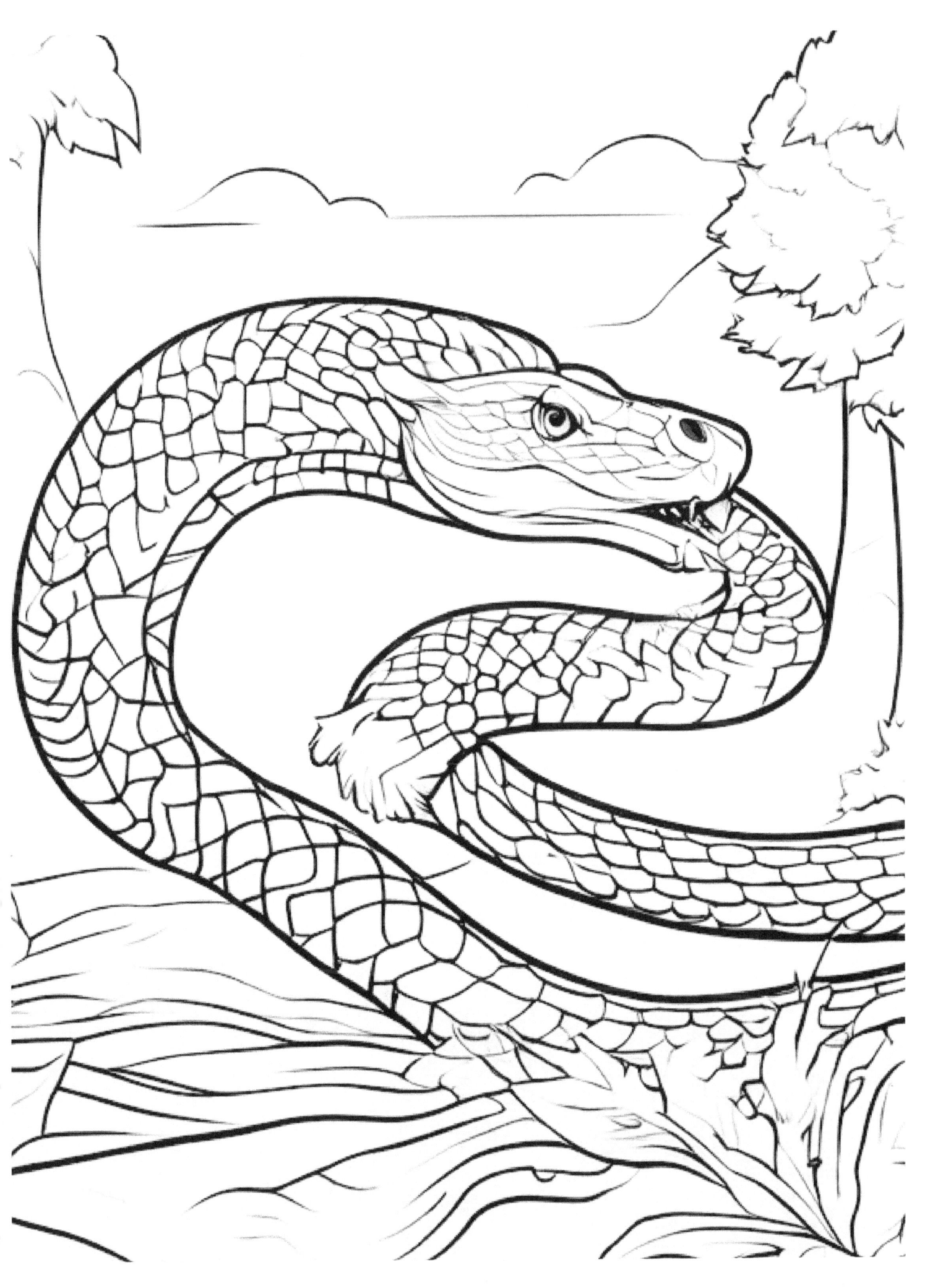

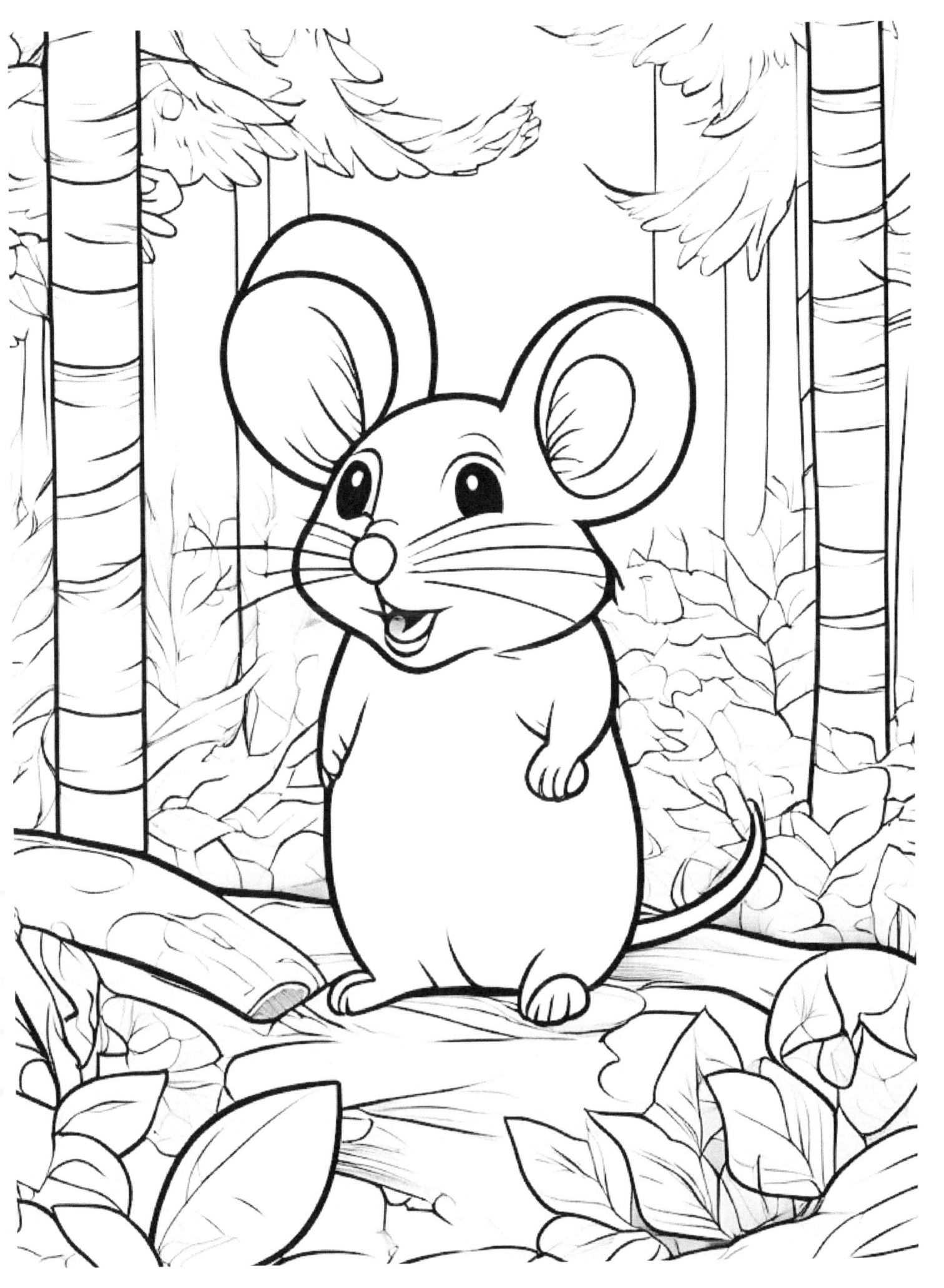

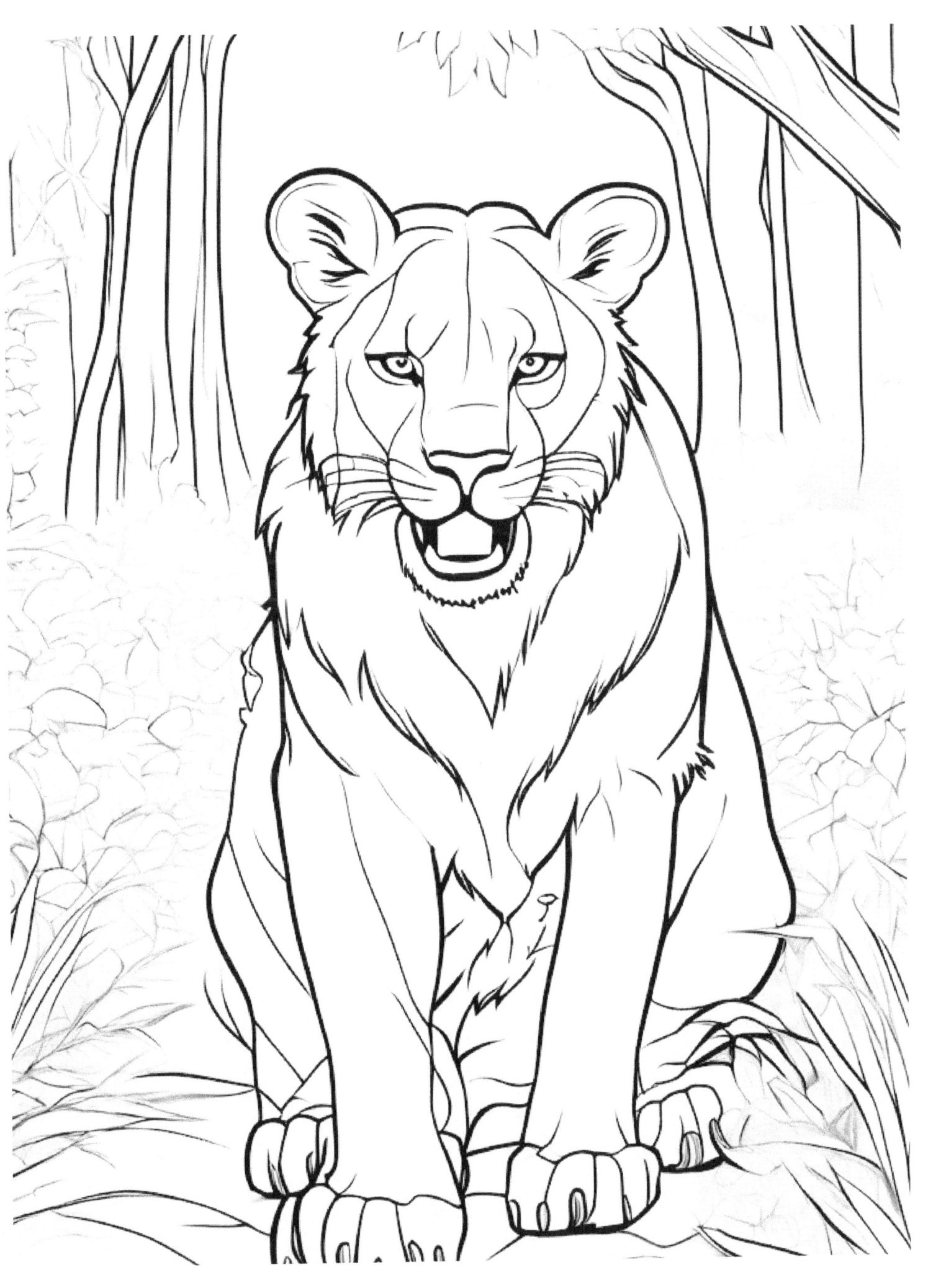

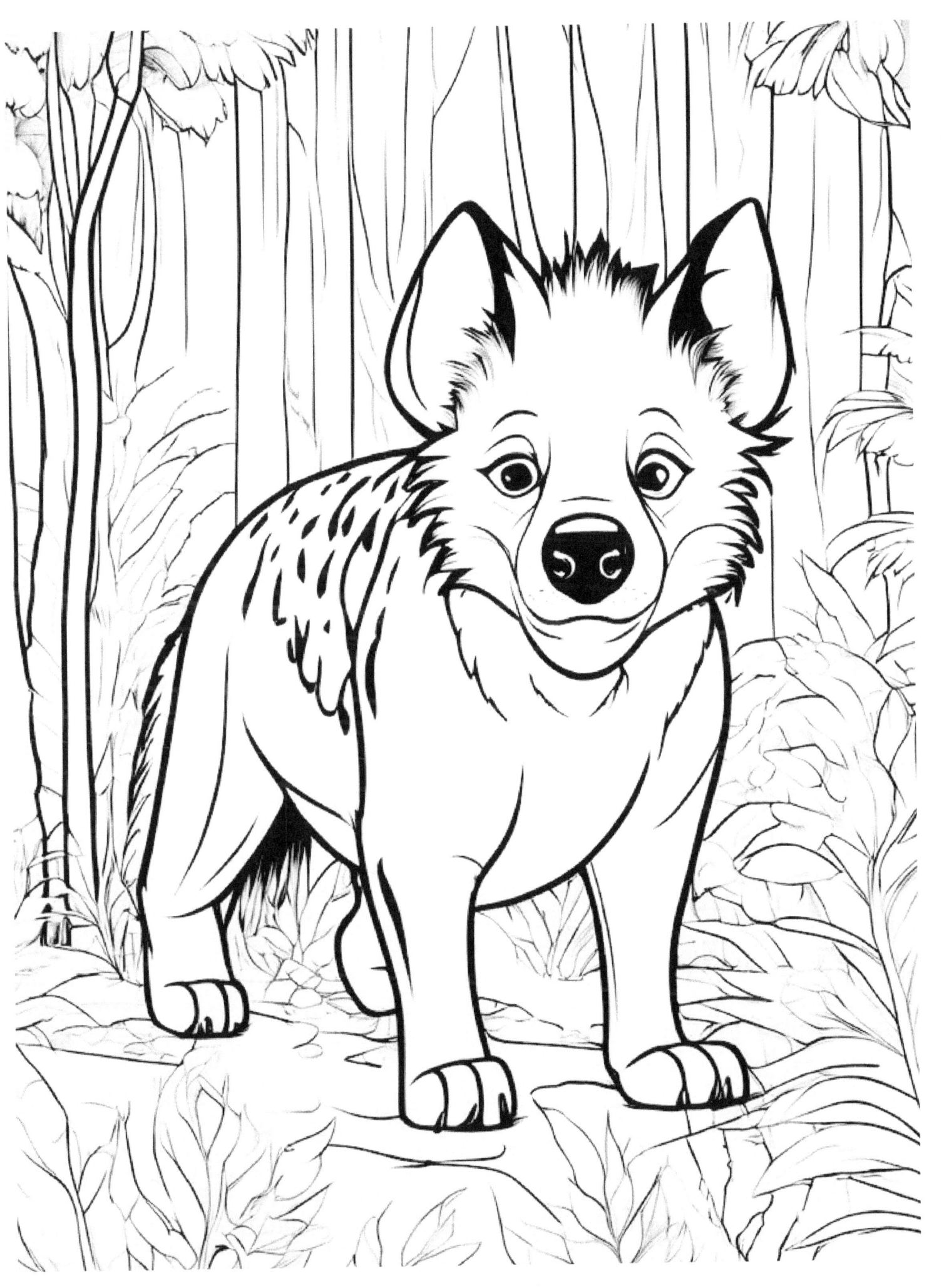

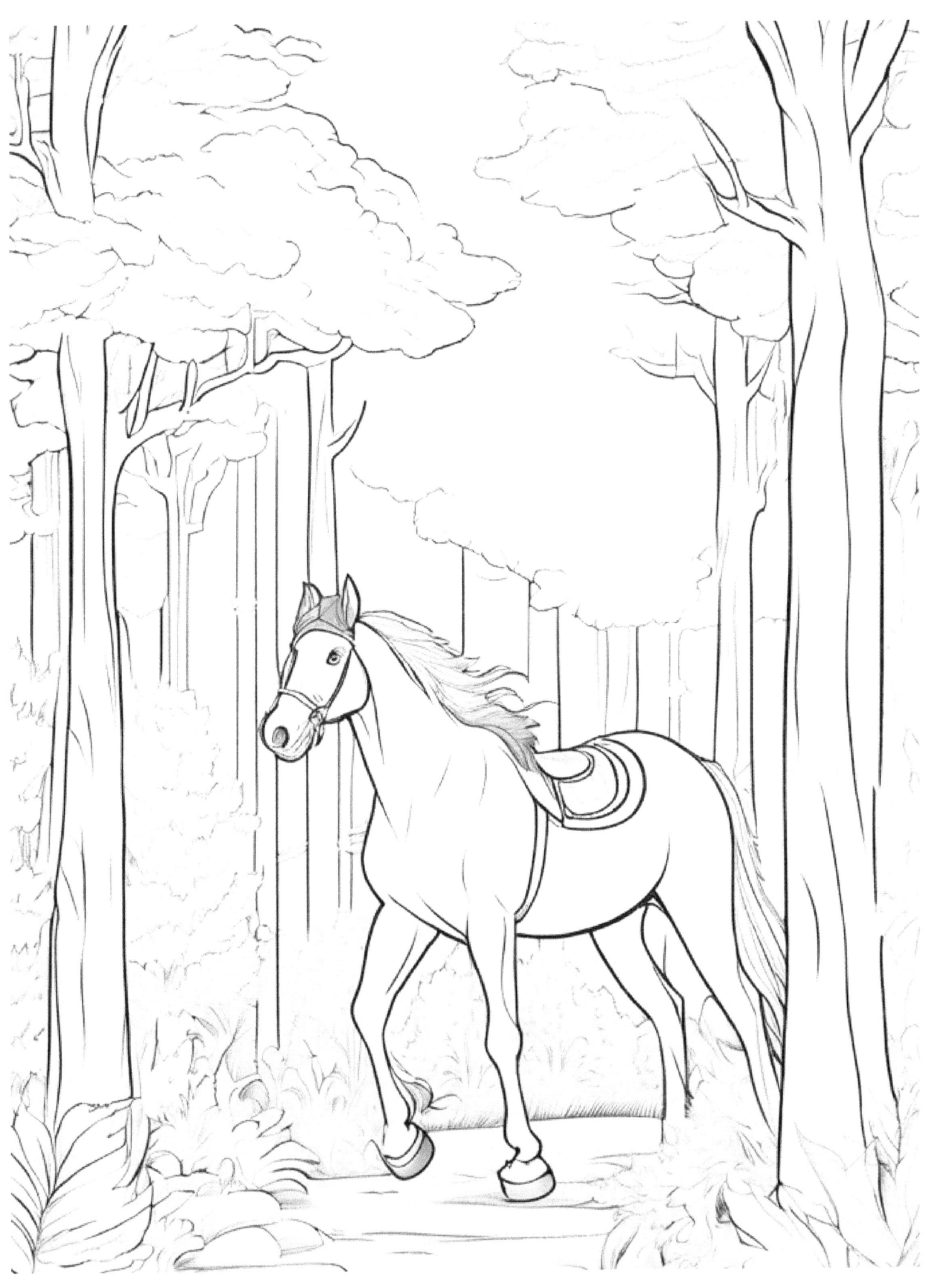

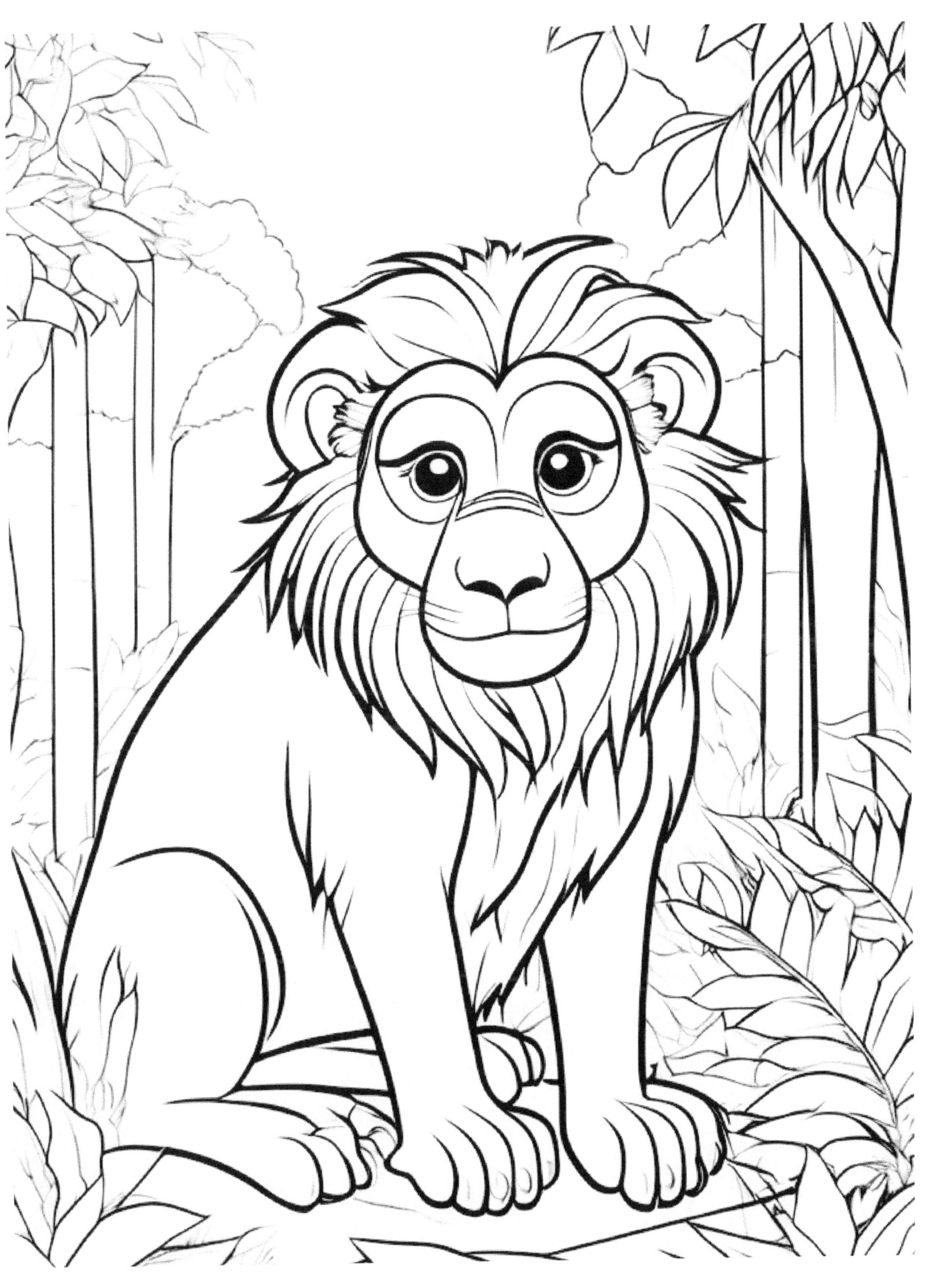

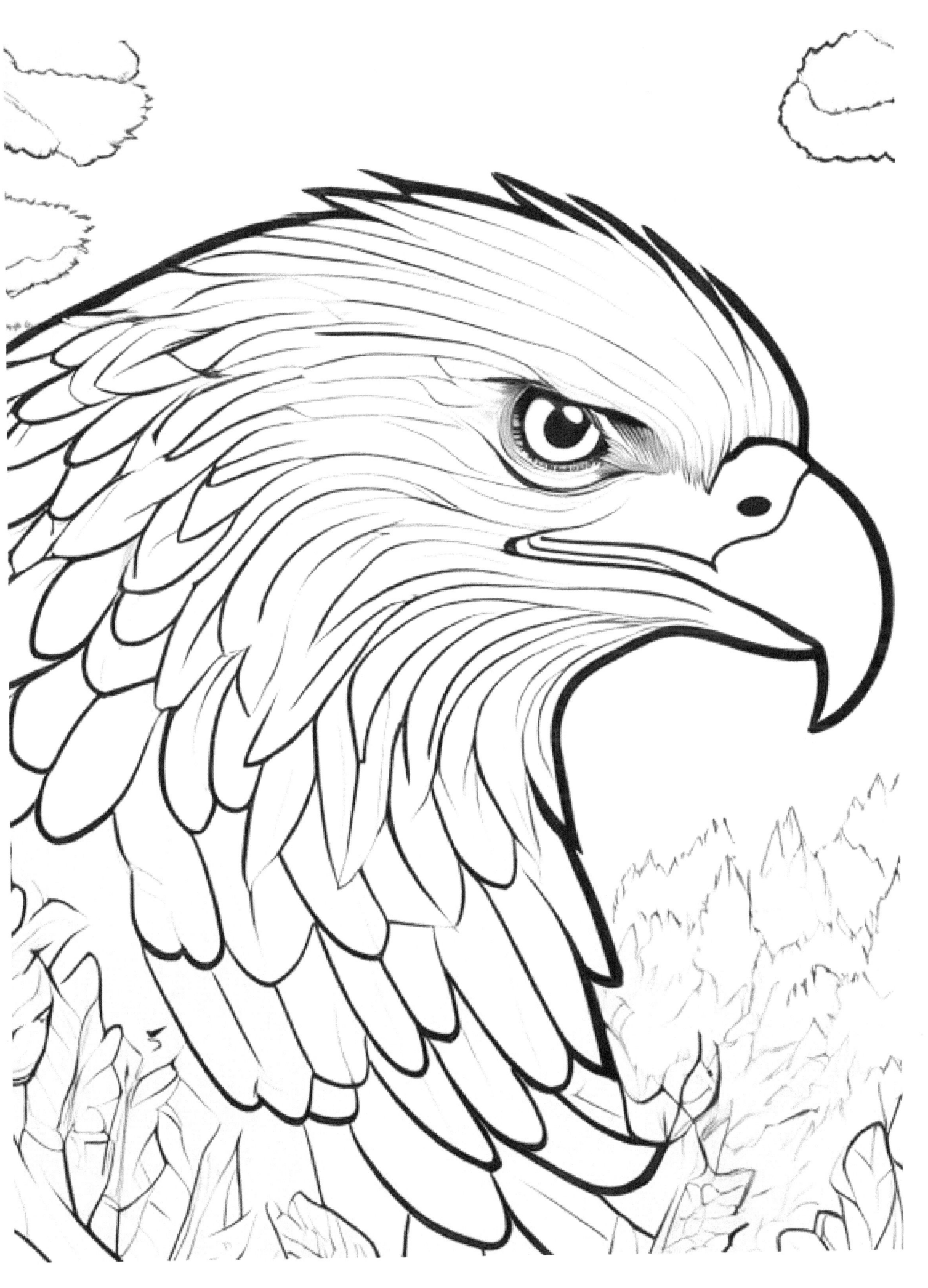

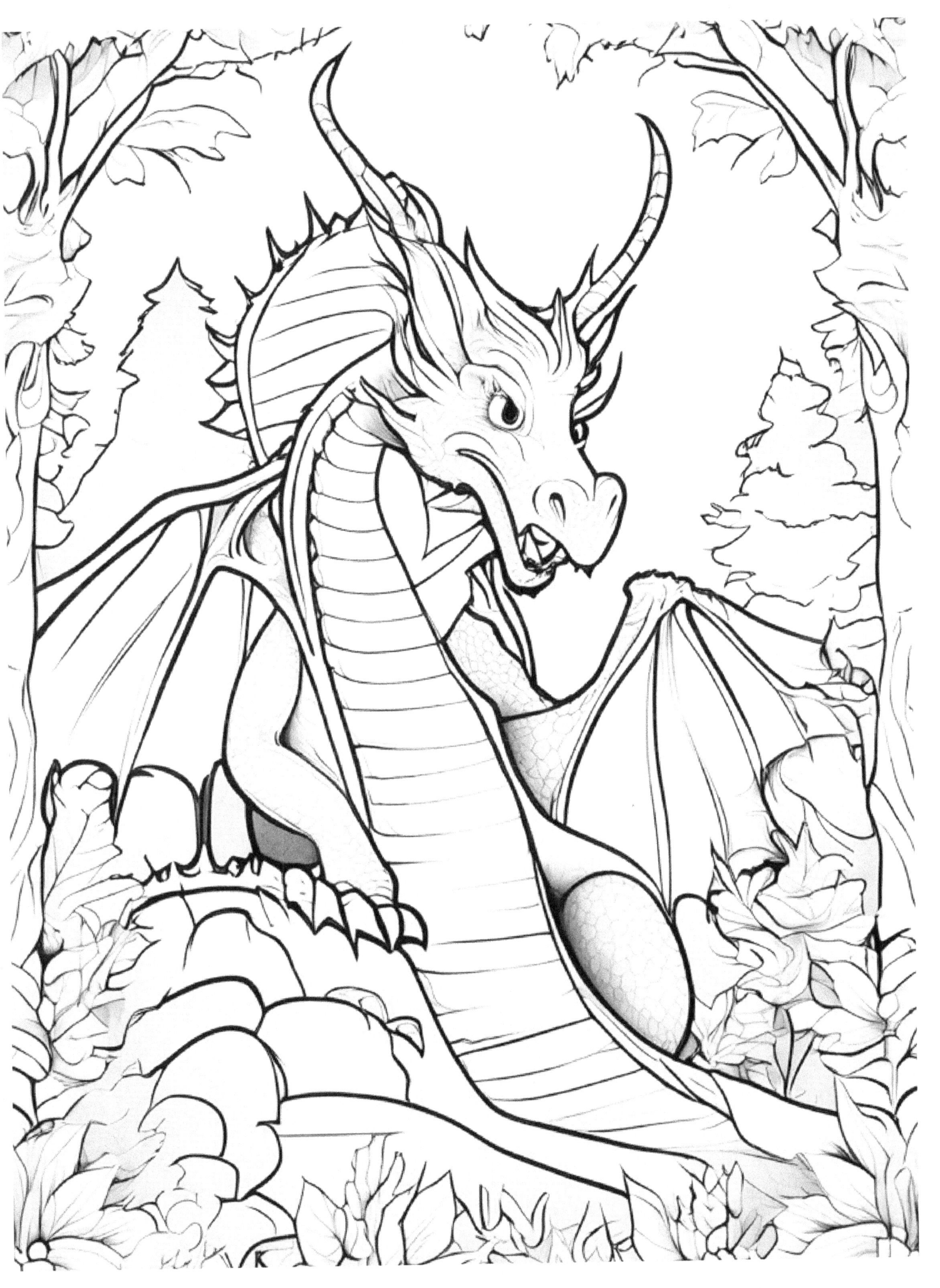

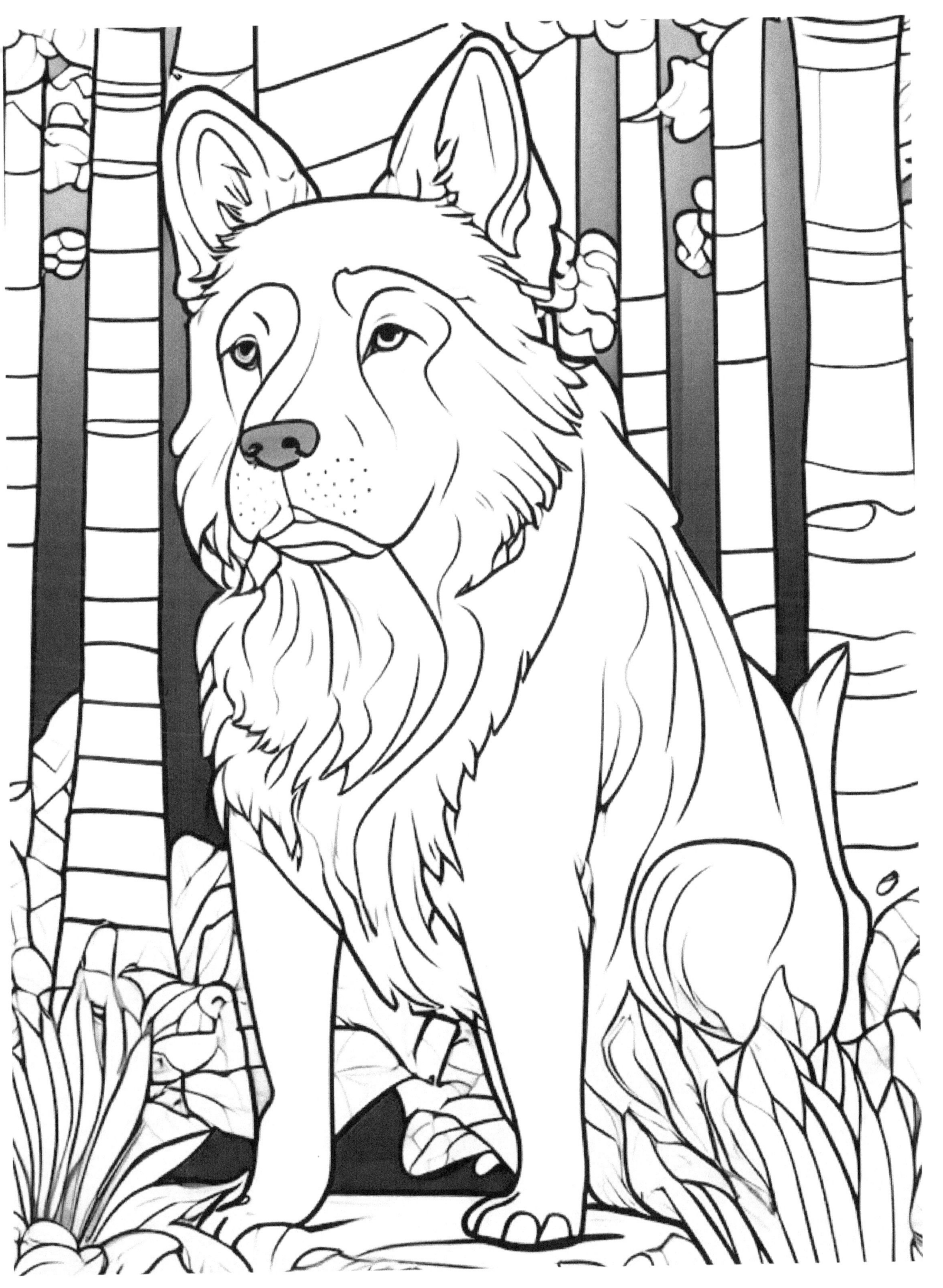

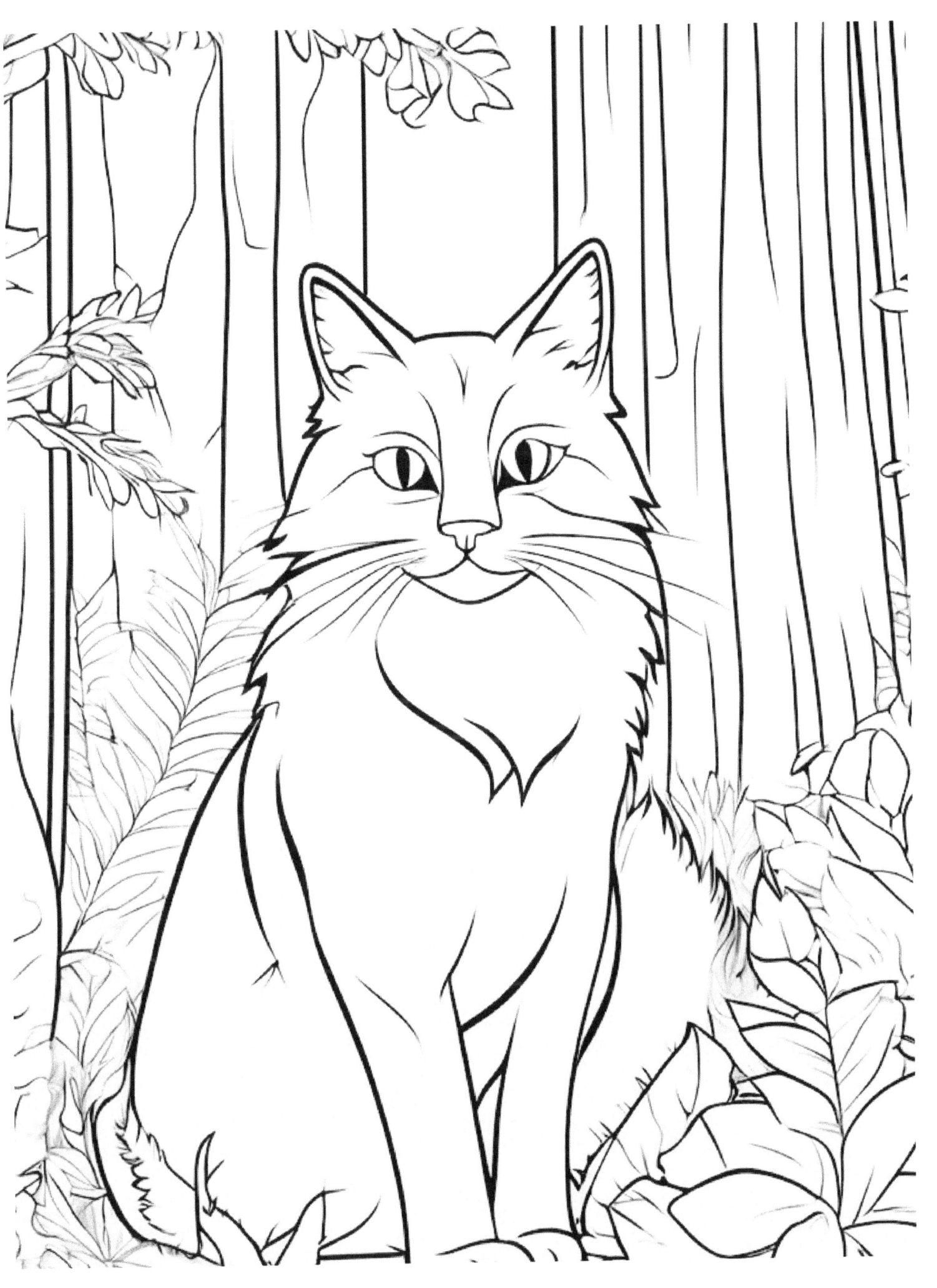

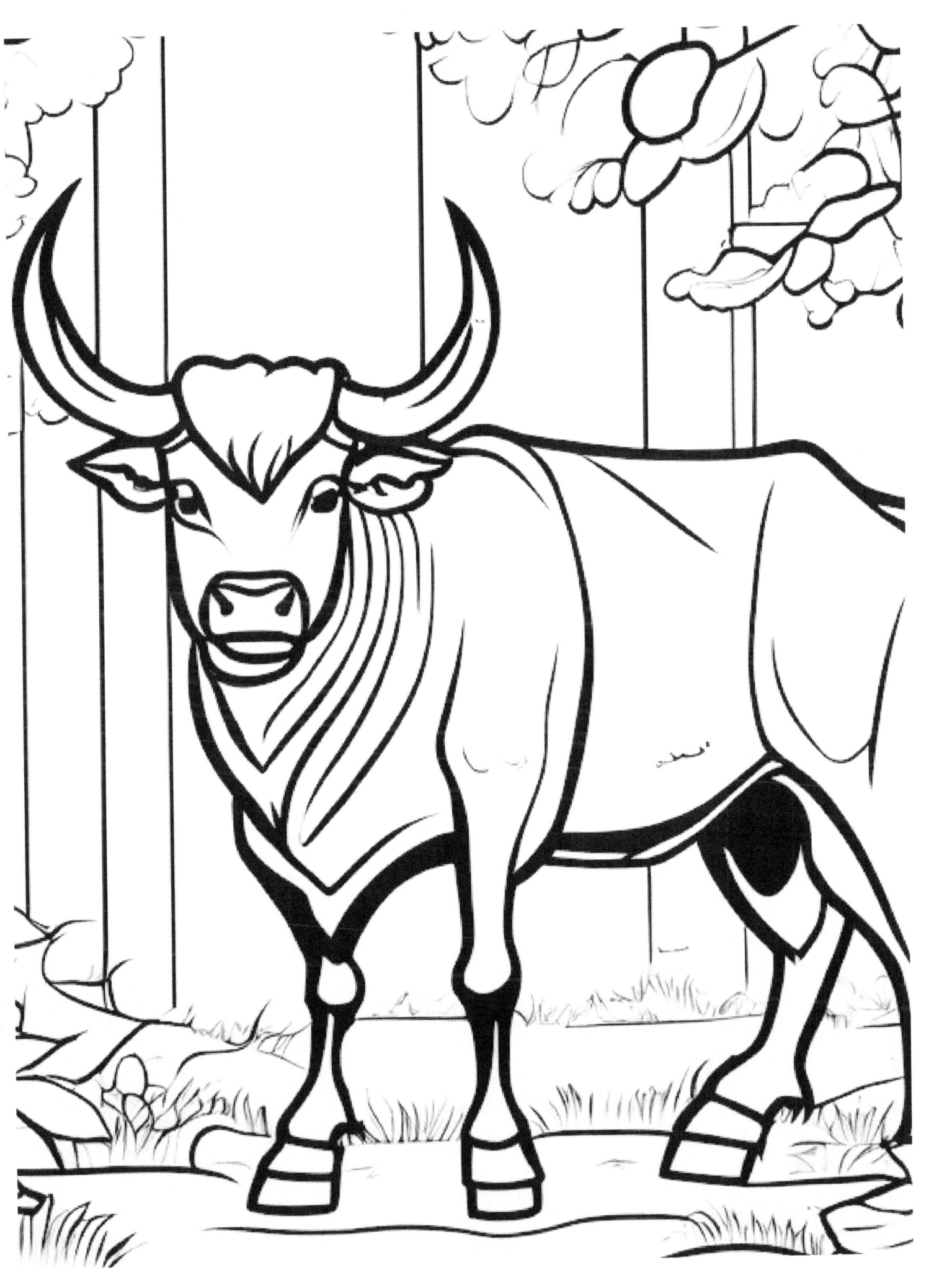

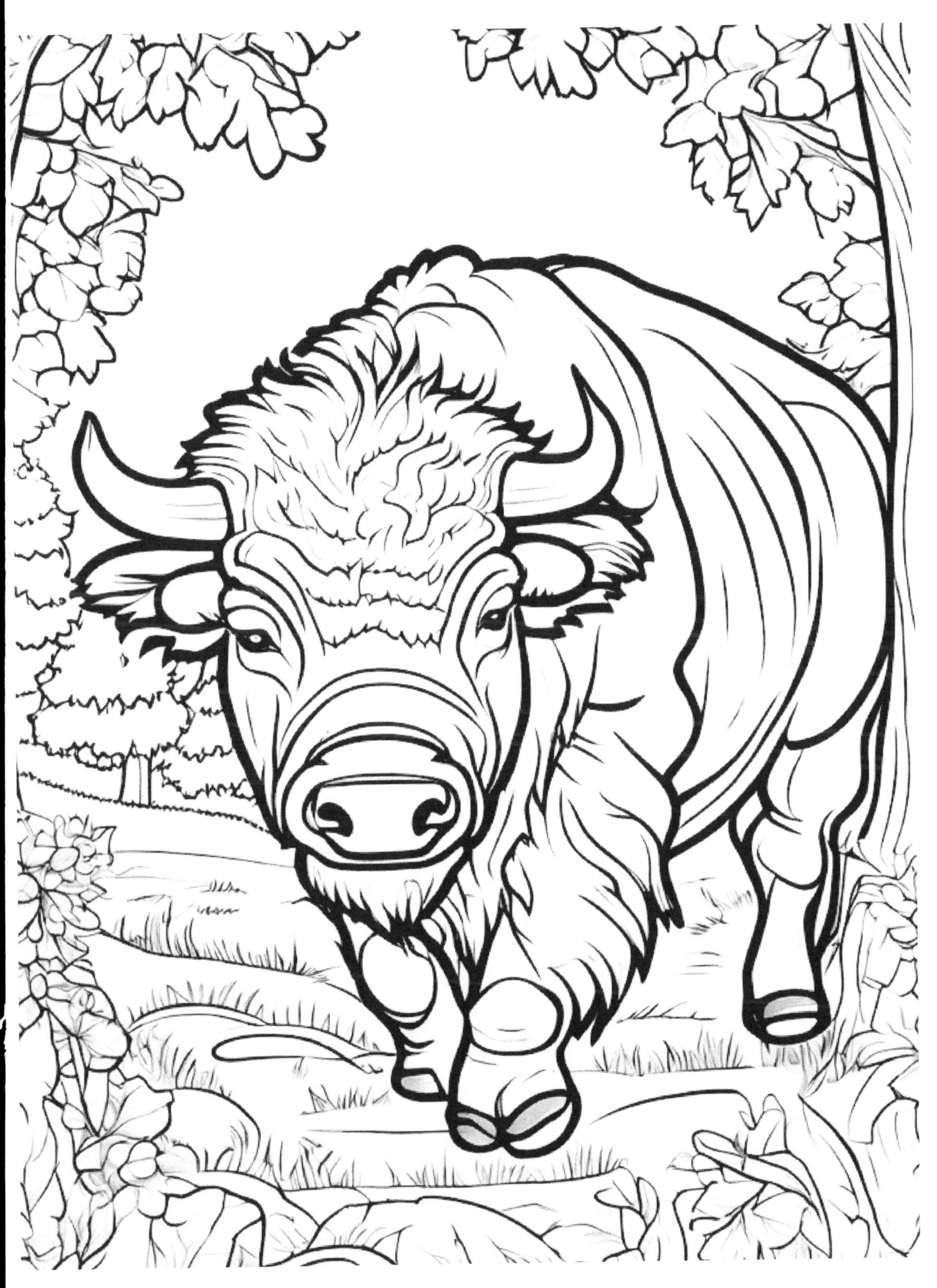

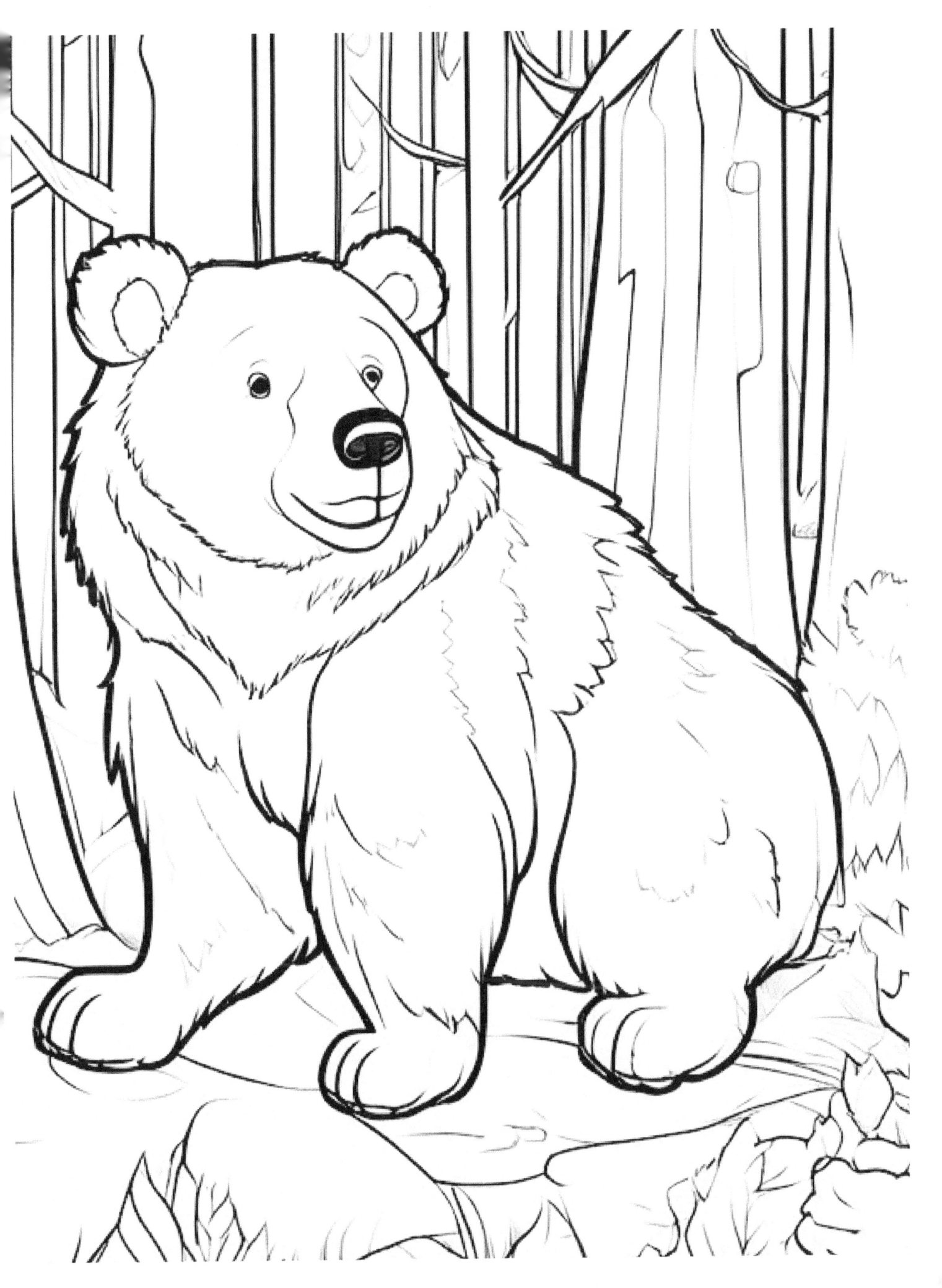

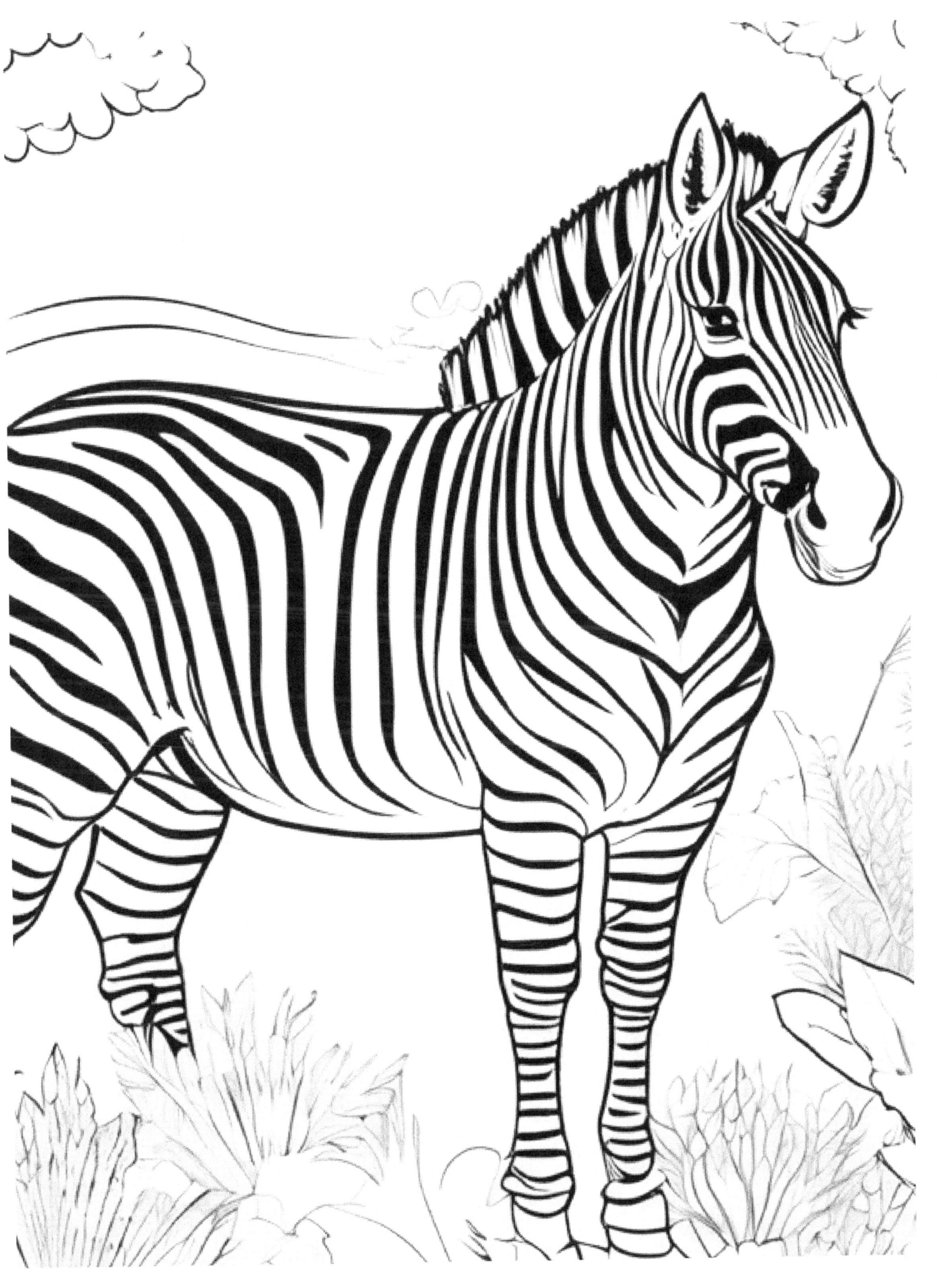

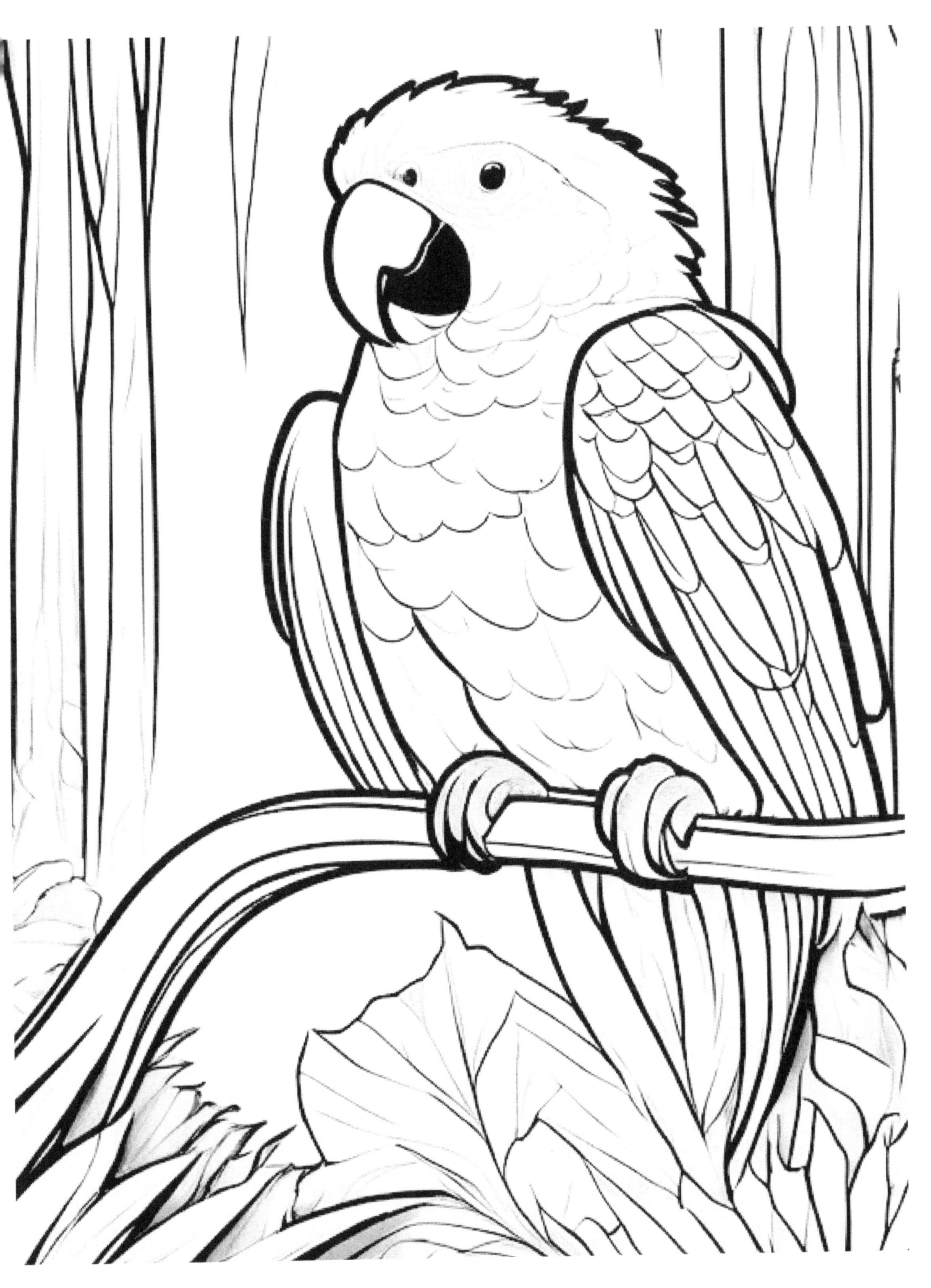

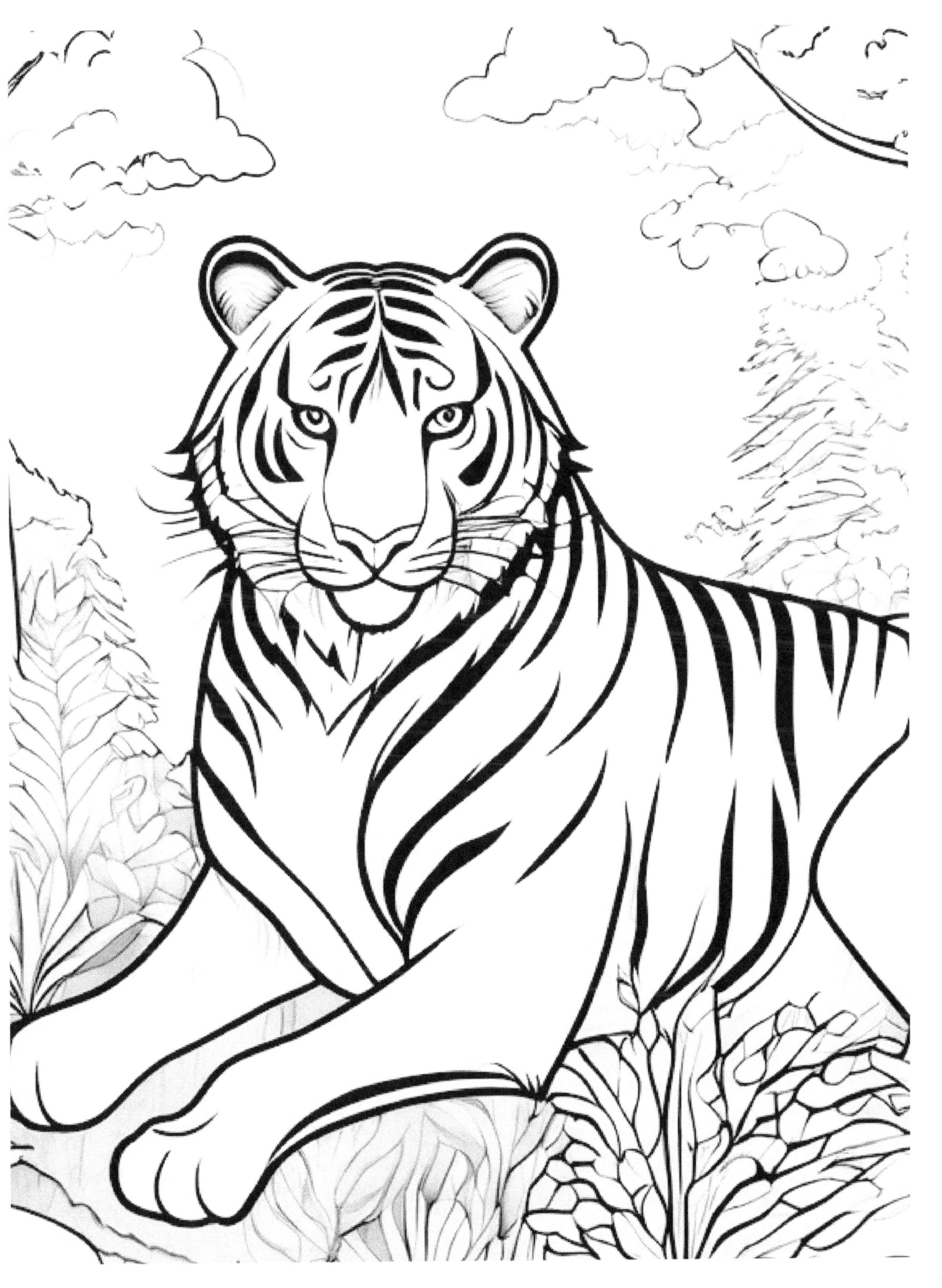

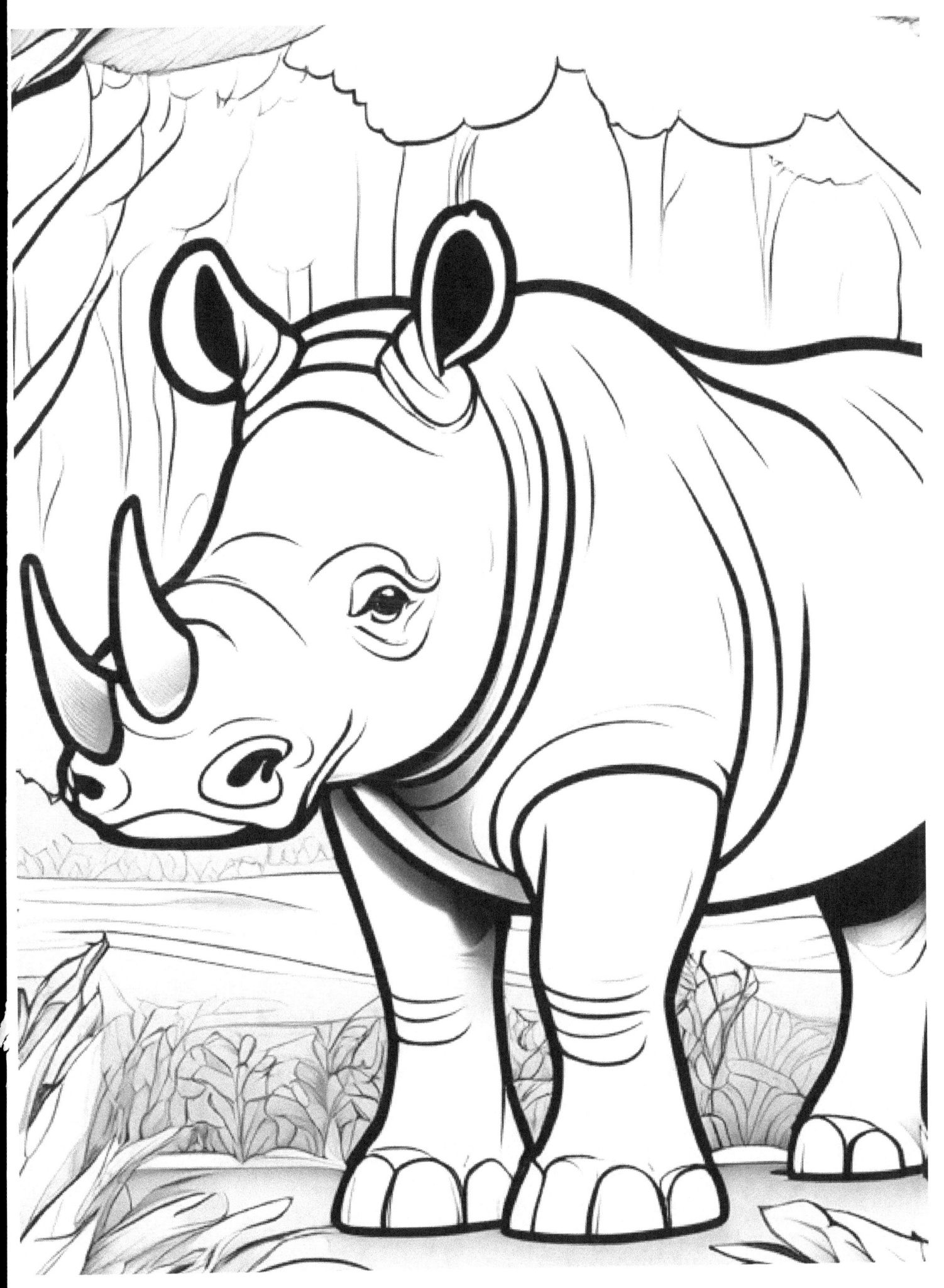

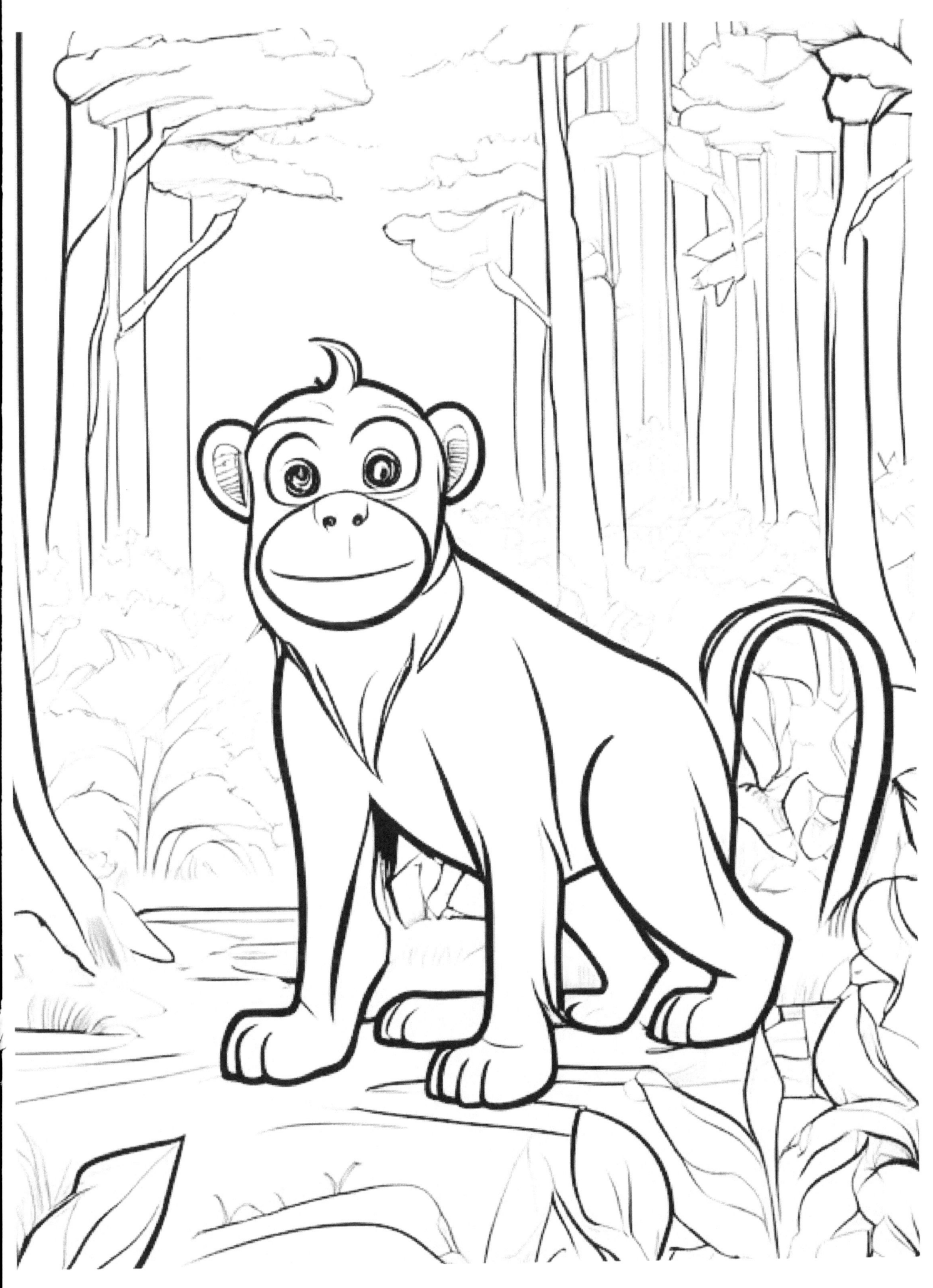

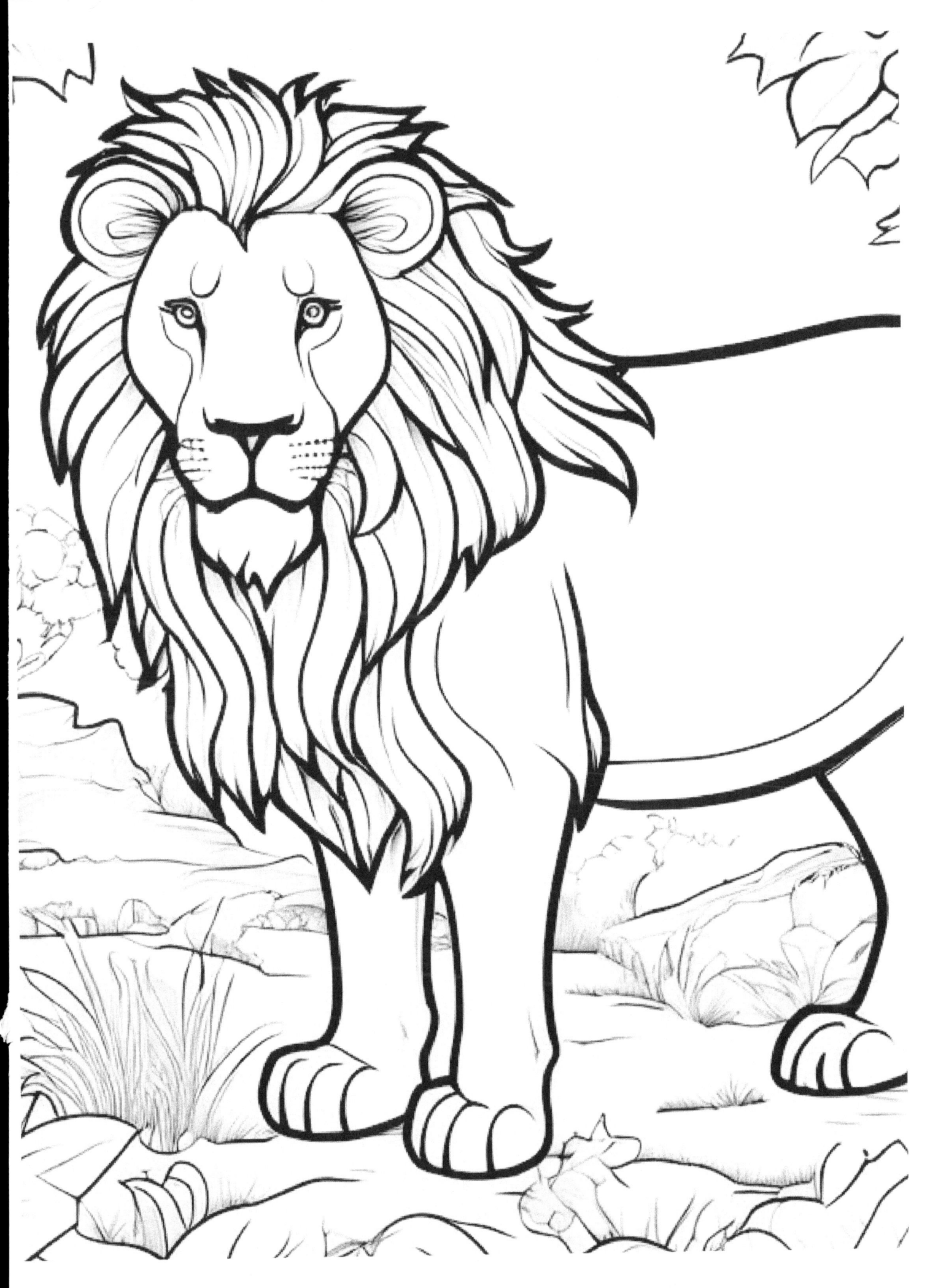

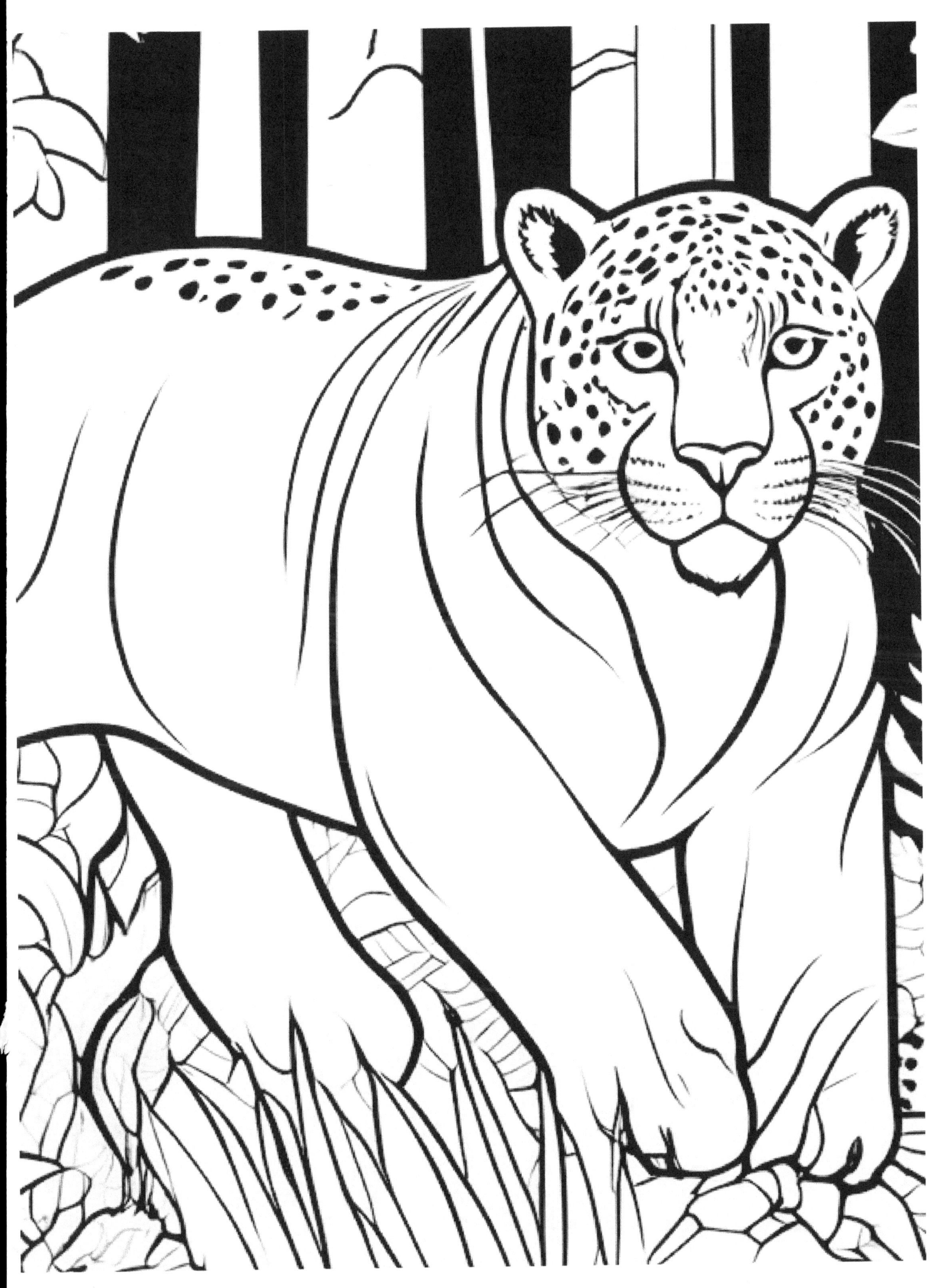

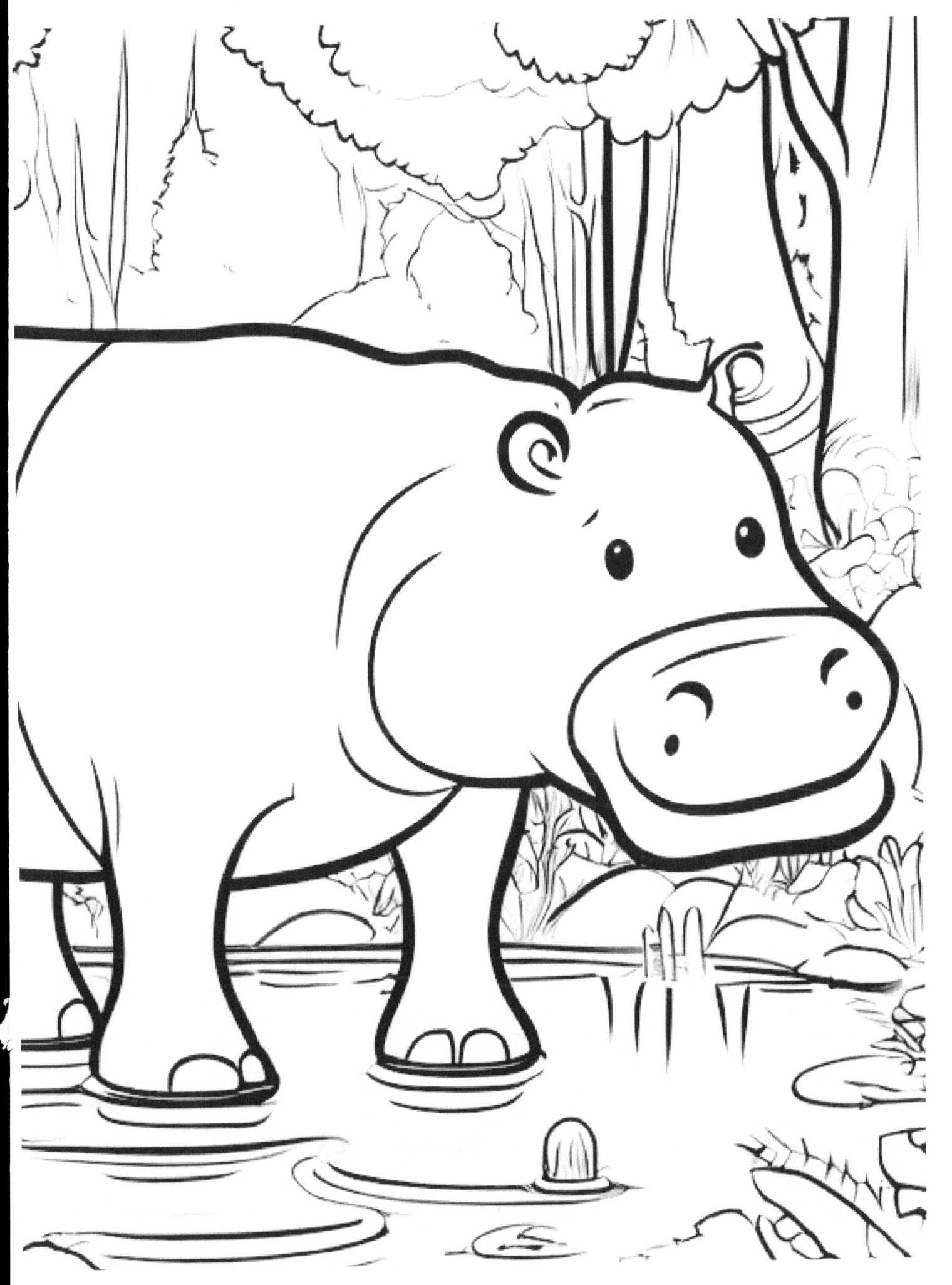

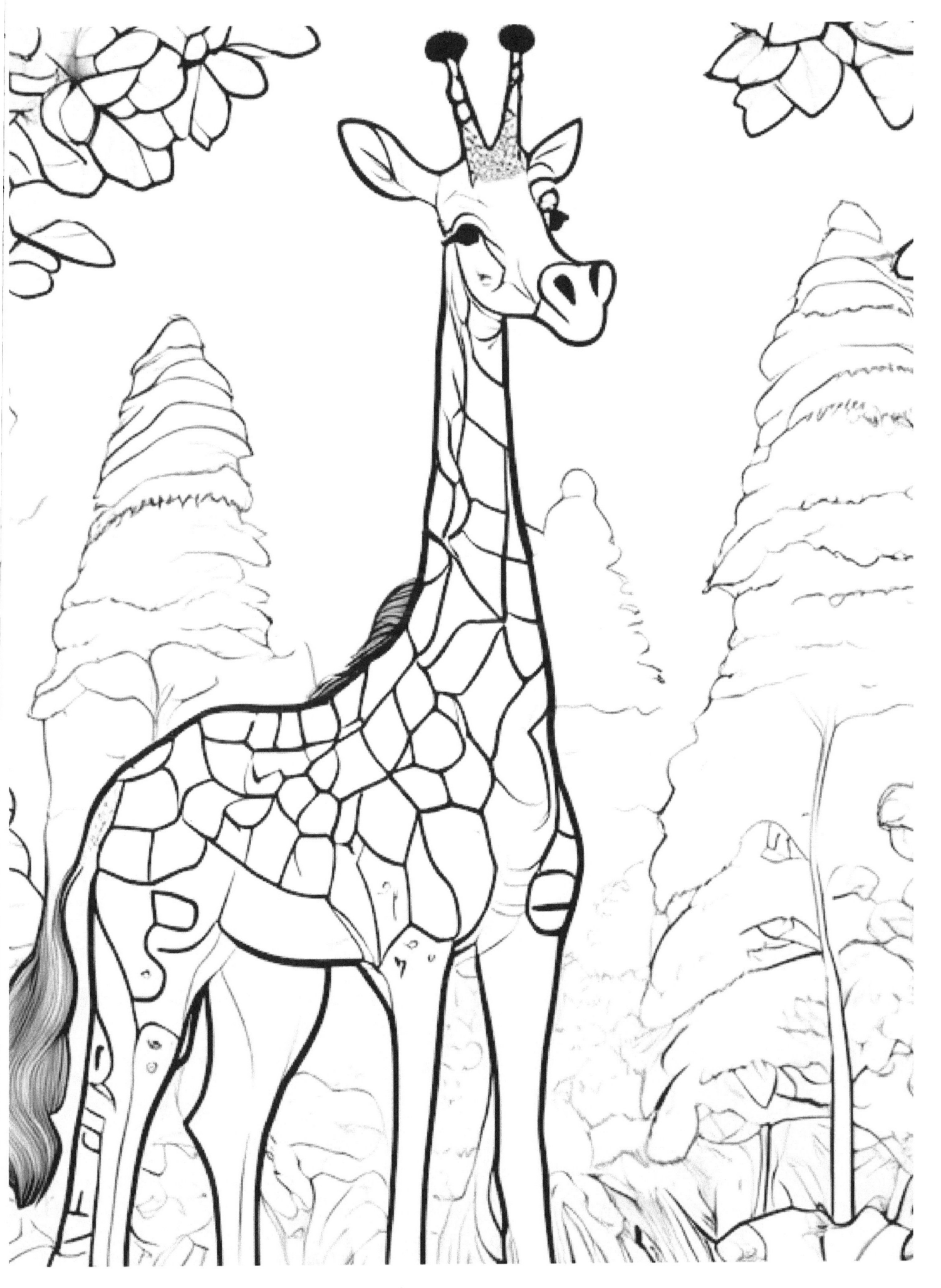

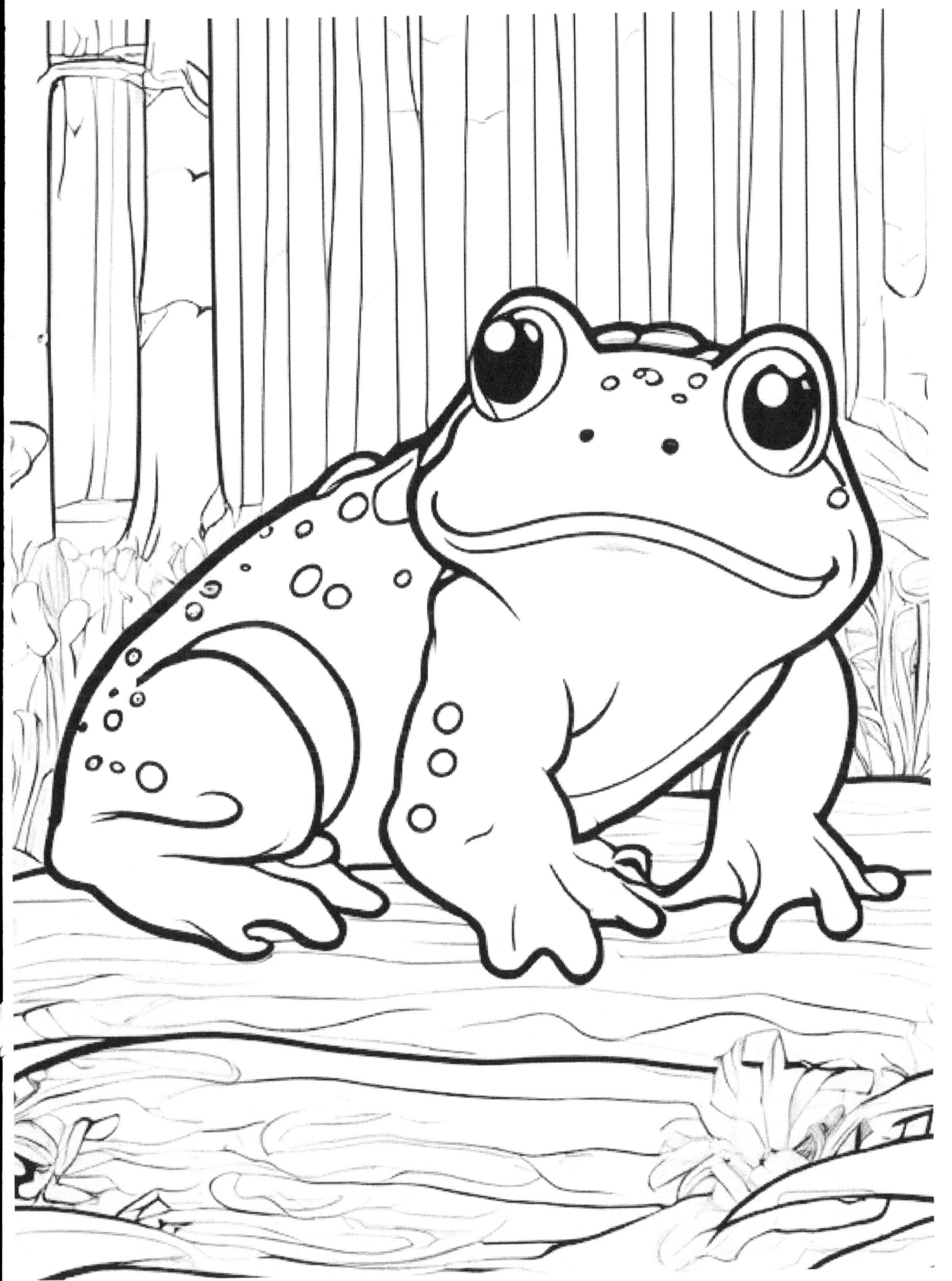

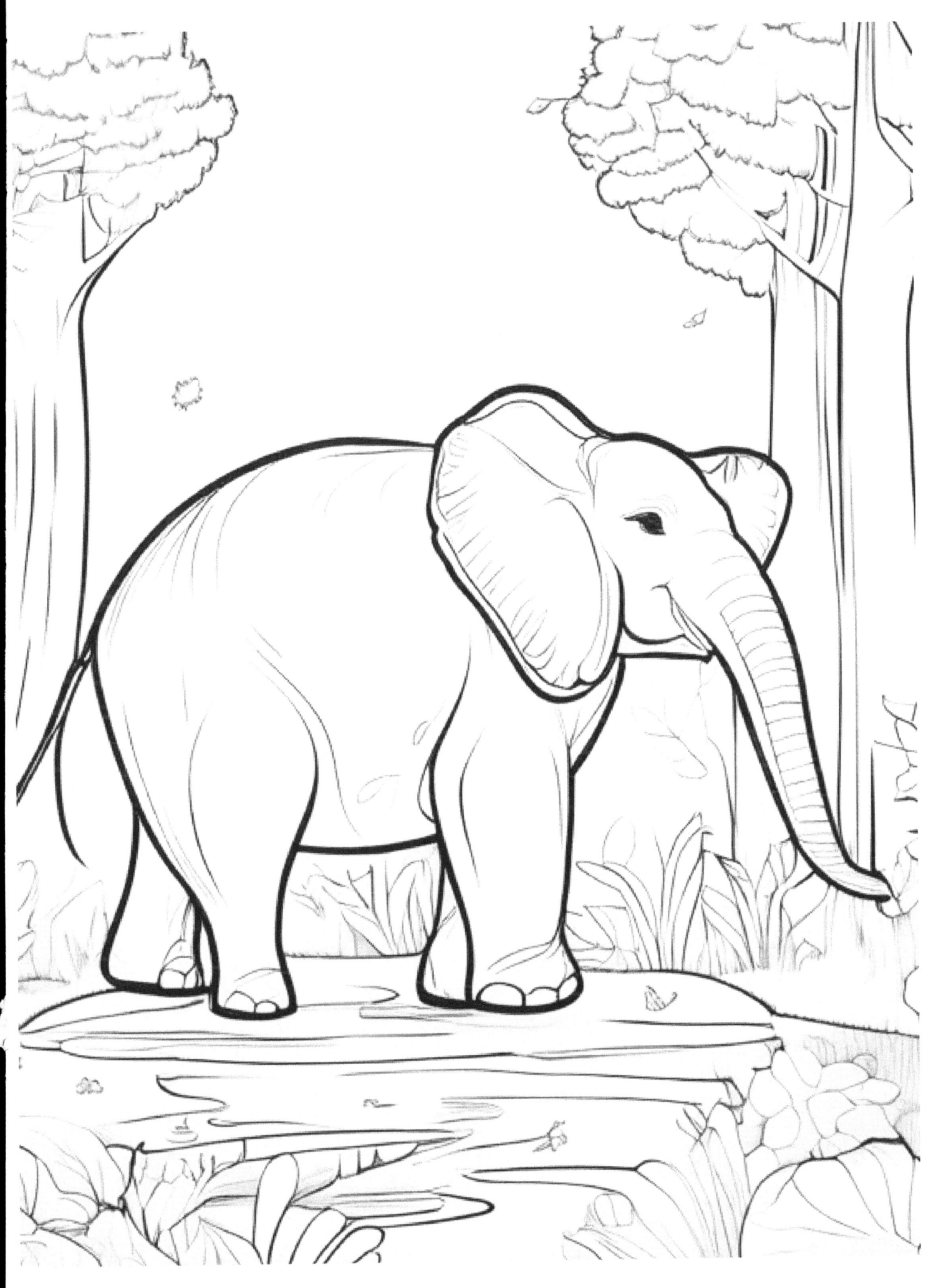

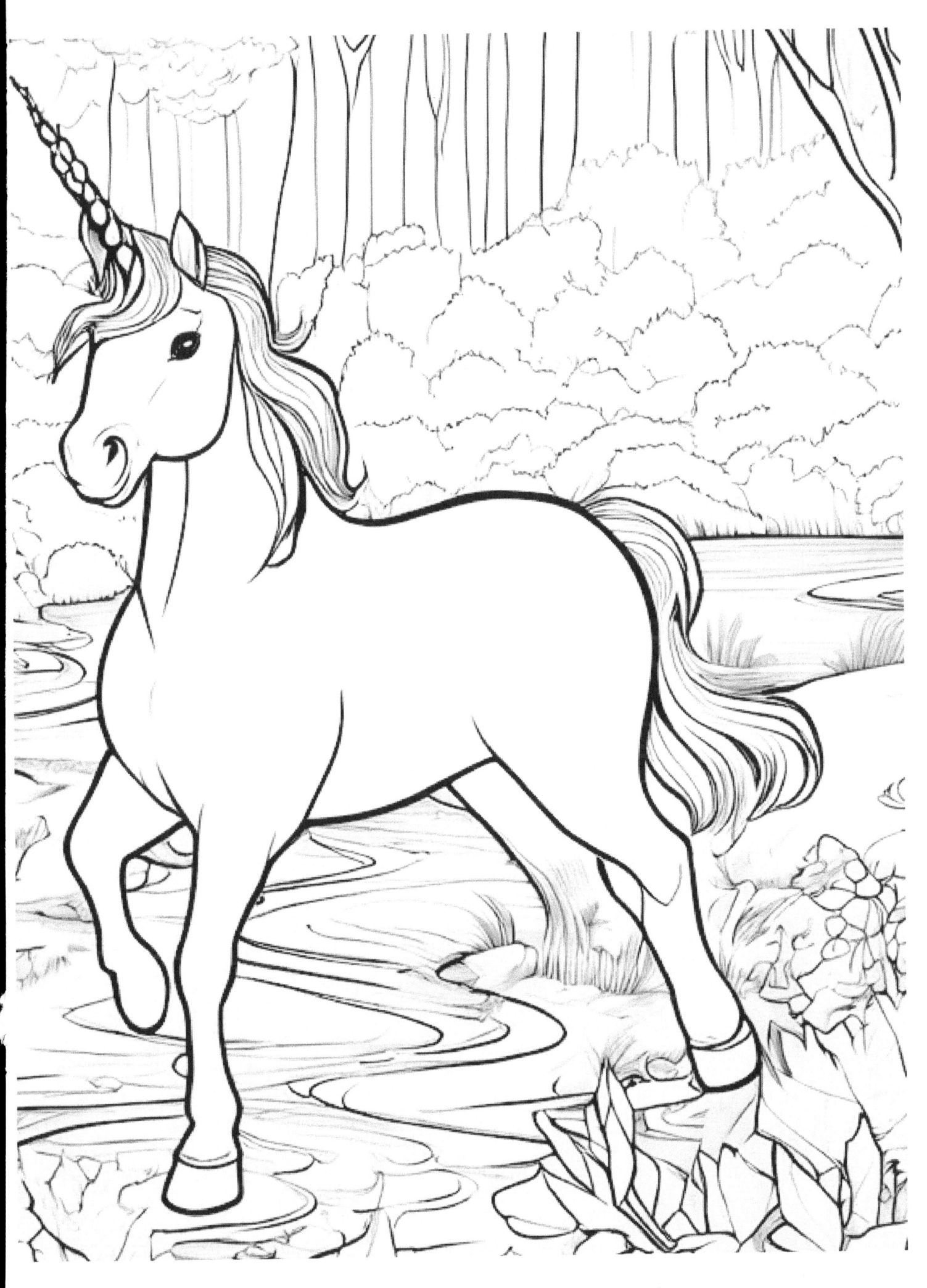

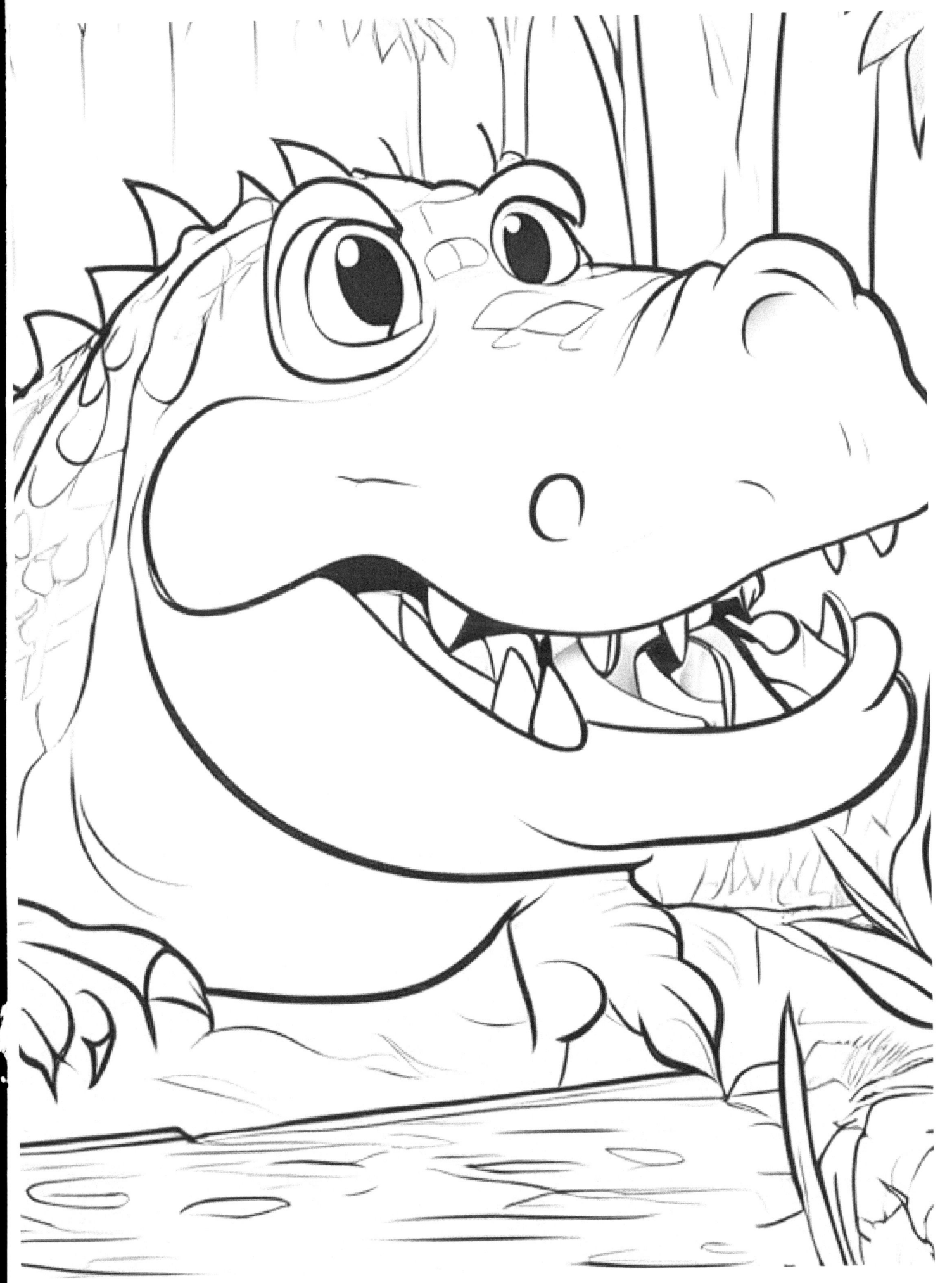

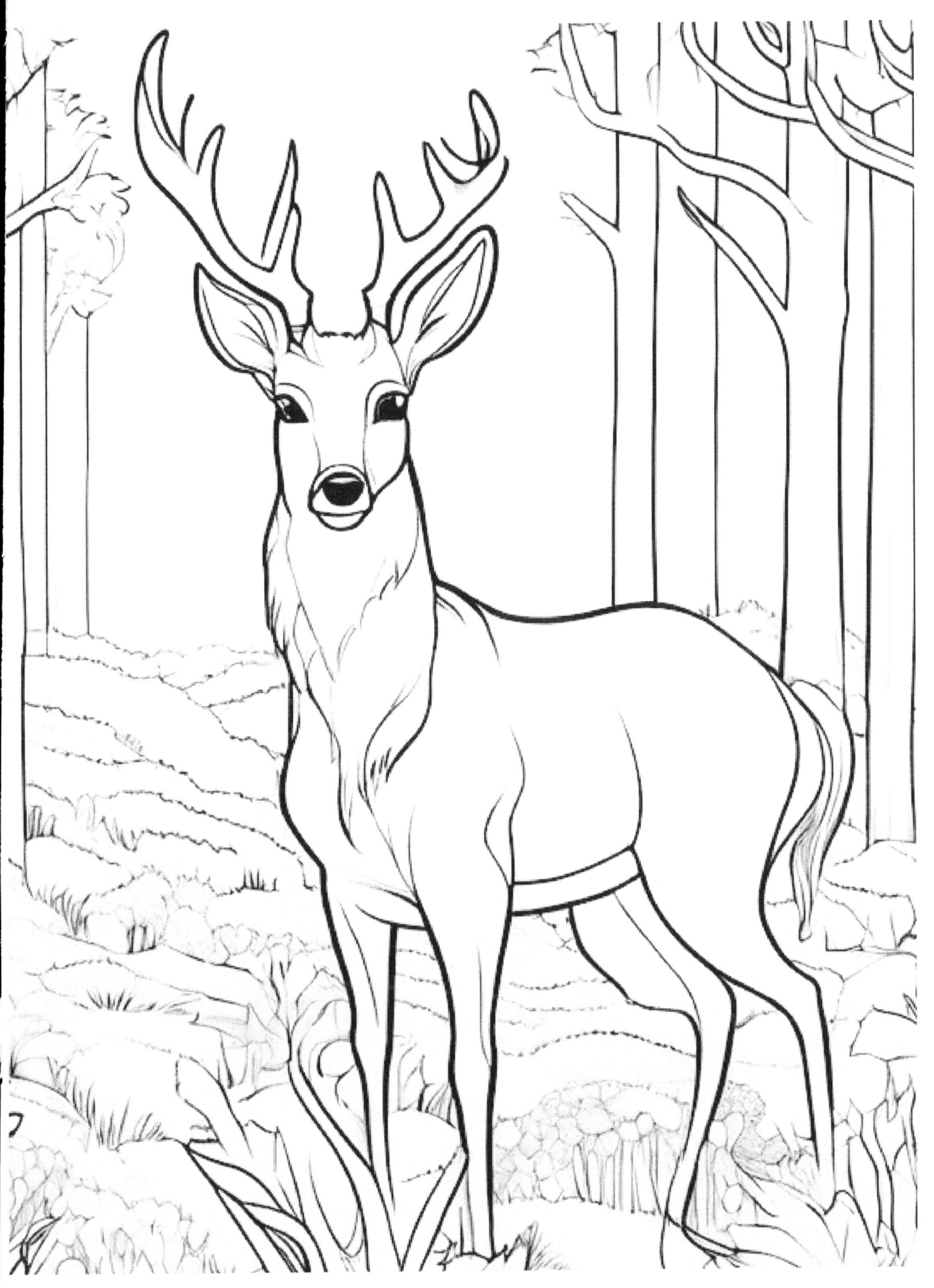